VOLUME 2

Books by Douglas Jacoby
Available from DPI

The God Who Dared: Genesis from Creation to Babel

Life to the Full: The Practical and Powerful Writings of James, Peter, John and Jude

Q & A: Answers to Bible Questions You Have Asked

Shining Like Stars: The Evangelism Handbook for the New Millennium

The Spirit: The Work of the Holy Spirit in the Lives of Disciples

True and Reasonable: Reasons for Faith in an Age of Doubt

More
Answers
to Bible
Questions
You
Have
Asked

Volume 2

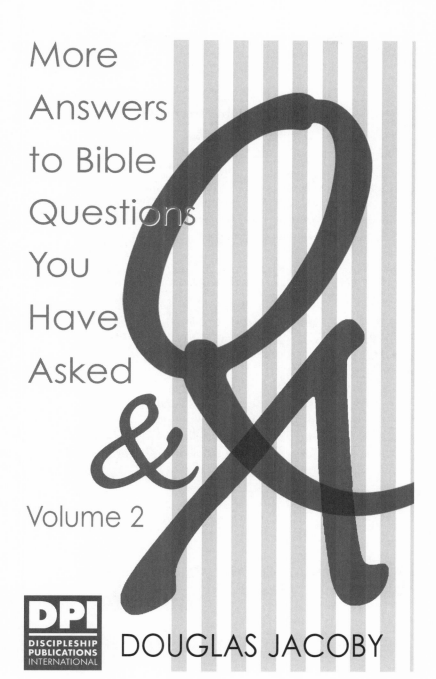

DPI
DISCIPLESHIP
PUBLICATIONS
INTERNATIONAL

DOUGLAS JACOBY

Q & A, Volume 2
© 2002 by Discipleship Publications International
2 Sterling Road, Billerica, Mass. 01862-2595

Printed in the United States of America

ISBN: 1-57782-174-2

Cover and Interior Design: Christine Nolan and Tony Bonazzi

To Mike Fontenot—

Humble soul, man of conviction, comrade-in-arms.

Contents

Section 3

Section 5

Acknowledgments

Credit for the first volume of *Q & A: Answers to Bible Questions You Have Asked* went to Mike Taliaferro. In 1998 he persuaded me to take advantage of new technologies and launch a Q & A column, with a view to creating a book out of the correspondence. Credit for this second volume of *Q & A* must go to my readers worldwide. Your curiosity, persistence and search for truth have truly kept me on my toes. Thank you.

In addition, my DPI publishers have been terrific—so easy to work with, professional and willing to go the extra mile. May their ministry be widely and generously supported!

Publisher's Note

The majority of the questions answered in this book were originally answered in the author's column, *The Bible on Trial,* which has appeared on the Aces Online Web site. From time to time in this book, the author will reference additional material that can be found in the archives for this column. Simply go to www.Acesonline.org, clicking first on "Doug Jacoby." This will take you to the page for "The Bible on Trial." On this page, click on the "Questions and Answers" tab for the archived material.

The answers to the questions in this book should not be read as the official position of any church body or of this publisher. They represent the opinion of one careful student of the Scriptures who knows that there may be other answers to many of these questions.

Abbreviations and Frequently Cited Works

Born of Water	Rex Geissler, *Born of Water: What the Bible Really Says About Baptism* (Denver: Great Commission Illustrated, 1996)
Encyclopedia of Difficulties	Gleason Archer, *Encyclopedia of Bible Bible Difficulties* (Grand Rapids: Zondervan, 1982)
The God Who Dared	Douglas Jacoby, *The God Who Dared: Genesis from Creation to Babel* (Billerica, Mass.: DPI, 1997)
How to Read the Bible All Its Worth	Gordon D. Fee and Douglas Stuart, *for How to Read the Bible for All Its Worth: A Guide to Understanding the Bible* (Grand Rapids: Zondervan, 1993)
Life to the Full	Douglas Jacoby, *Life to the Full: Practical and Powerful Writings of James, Peter, John & Jude* (Billerica, Mass.: DPI, 1995)
NT	"New Testament" as an adjective
OT	"Old Testament" as an adjective
Q & A	Douglas Jacoby, *Q & A: Answers to Bible Questions You Have Asked* (Billerica, Mass.: DPI, 2001)
Shining Like Stars	Douglas Jacoby, *Shining Like Stars: The Evangelism Handbook for the New Millennium,* revised and expanded (Billerica, Mass.: DPI, 2000)
The Spirit	Douglas Jacoby, *The Spirit: The Work of the Holy Spirit in the Lives of Disciples* (Billerica, Mass.: DPI, 1998)
When Critics Ask	Norman Geisler and Thomas Howe, *When Critics Ask: A Comprehensive Handbook on Bible Difficulties* (Wheaton, Il.: Victor Books, 1992)

Introduction

Hunger and Thirst

All over the world, in every nation and among every population segment, people have questions—they are hungry for God and thirsty for truth. This is because God created us human beings as spiritual creatures and intellectual ones.

Being *spiritual* creatures means that life simply does not make sense without God in the picture. As humans have drifted away from God, our perspective has become skewed. What would otherwise be clear is now distorted, confusing. As someone said, "There is an empty space in our hearts, and only God can fill it." We hunger for God because he made us spiritual—and something is missing without him (Ecclesiastes 3:11).

Being intellectual creatures, regardless of our level of education, means that we all think, reflect and explore. We are somewhat restless until we receive answers to our questions. We thirst for truth.

Yes, we hunger and thirst. I know this because I myself am hungry and thirsty. I love to read and I thrill at the chance to listen to another's wisdom, to consider his thoughts. I also know this to be the case because I travel and speak rather extensively. From Africa to the South Pacific, from South America to Asia, from North America to Europe, those I speak with—as a preacher and teacher—are hungry and thirsty. I see it in their eyes and hear it in their voices. Very often, after a lesson, we "open it up" for a time of questioning. Common questions focus on God, science, church history, evidences, the problem of suffering, difficult Bible passages and many other areas of inquiry. And when one hand goes up, even in a group of thousands, I know that many others who have not raised their hands share the same question—or questions like it. Any occasion to address common questions and concerns is a fabulous teaching opportunity.

The Book of Answers?

Perhaps this deep hunger and thirst is why the first volume, *Q & A: Answers to Bible Questions You Have Asked* met with such an eager reception. Shortly before it was published, someone suggested, "Doug, why don't you write a book discussing every doctrine and every possible question? It would be a big book, but then there would only be one book that we would need to consult to figure out the truth!" My reply was not very enthusiastic. In fact, I was somewhat horrified. "What—you want me to write a book with all the answers so you won't need to read the Bible?! The Bible is supposed to be the one book you need. Besides, what makes you think *my* answers would necessarily be the right ones?"

The man who made the suggestion, and the entire group listening, got the point. After all, how would this make us any different from those who say, "You don't need to read the Bible; just trust the priests. They have studied, ask them"? The Bible and the Bible alone is the authority and the source of truth. Watch out for shortcuts, gimmicks and even *books* that claim to eliminate the need for serious personal study.

Let's not be deceived about this. Even trying to produce an exhaustive "Answer Book" would be both unrealistic and counterproductive (as well as "exhausting" for writer and reader alike!). The goal of teaching is not merely to supply information but to teach us how to think.

This book does not aim to be comprehensive, only to provide a sampling of answers to questions and to illustrate ways we can find solutions to problems. Again, *Q & A, Volume 2* is written not so much to give answers—despite the somewhat misleading (if memorable) title—as to enable us to arrive at the truth ourselves through considering new approaches, new angles, new perspectives. It is written to enable us to become and remain *learners*.

Mathetai

There are many names in the Bible for a follower of Jesus Christ, for example: "believer," "brother," "saint," "Christian," "friend" and "disciple." Each word emphasizes a different aspect of our common experience or attitude in Christ. The word translated as "disciple" in the Greek New Testament is *mathetes* (mah-they-TES). What does this mean? *Mathetes* comes from the verb *manthanein*, "to learn." *Mathetai* (plural) are learners. The lexicon defines "disciple" as "learner, student, pupil, apprentice." All these meanings are reasonable translations.

Are you a learner? Some Christians think they are too old to be learners or students. And yet we see in God's word that if we are not learners, we are not really followers of Jesus Christ. Each one of us is called—regardless of age, gender, education or culture—to be a student: students of human nature and the world around us, keen observers of character, men and women eager to learn everything possible from anything and anybody and above all, avid students of the Word.

Are you accurately described as a "student"? This is not the only aspect of Biblical Christianity—hopefully you are also a true believer, a loyal brother, a devoted saint and a caring friend—but it is certainly a fundamental one. Being a learner means that we pose questions, that we seek answers.

All of us are questioners. We were born to wonder, to ask, to seek. When we stop questioning, we stop learning. When we stop learning, we stop growing in Christ.

How to Use This Book

Like the first volume, *Q & A, Volume 2* is divided into five sections. It is not necessarily a book you will want to read straight through (though many of you will choose to do it this way).

Section 1   Crucial Issues
Section 2   Difficult Passages
Section 3   Basic Bible
Section 4   Various and Sundry
Section 5   Essays

Feed Yourself!

At this point let me offer some advice for anyone seeking answers to Bible questions. If you follow these words of wisdom, in the end you will be a sharper thinker, better able to help others to know the Lord. (And those you might otherwise have plied with questions will be grateful!) The point is to do your best before relying on others for insight.

- Try to figure out the difficulty or question yourself, using whatever Bible tools you have. Read books.

Aim to teach and train yourself (Joshua 1:8, 2 Timothy 2:15, Hebrews 5:11–14). Build your own theological library. (Everybody has one—the question is, what's in it? Is your library abundant or sparse? Are the volumes shallow or deep? Do they call you to think and stretch you, or do they only gently restate what you already believe?)

- If you still need help, ask your friends for ideas, leads or reading suggestions. Often your questions were others' questions. Why reinvent the wheel or waste the opportunity to benefit from valuable lessons they have learned?

- If this does not bring the insight you seek, then speak with your ministry leaders. Generally speaking, the more experienced they are, the better prepared they will be to assist you with your questions.

- If your leaders are stumped, perhaps speak with or e-mail someone outside your local congregation. Yet, again, this should be a last resort, not a shortcut in place of personal study.

- Be patient. Sometimes you will not be able to understand the answer to a question until you have spent many years walking with the Lord and poring over his word. God will reveal his ways to you as you give your heart—and mind—to him. This takes time.

Chances are, if you follow this sequence, you will not only find guidance and build your confidence in God's word, but you will also become a better student of the Word. Remember, "disciple" means "learner"!

More Answers Than Questions

At the end of the day, there will always be more answers than we even have questions! That's because God already has the answers to every question we could possibly put to him, for he is the God of truth.

1
Crucial Issues

1. Why Did Jesus Come?

"Why did Jesus come to earth? Did he just come to improve our society?"

Excellent question! Why did he come? What was his mission on this earth? He came to reconcile man to God and to preach about this great news. In a word, his visit to our planet was about *salvation*. This salvation is not just from the punishment we deserve for our sins, but also from the "corrupt generation" we live in (Acts 2:40, 2 Peter 1:3–4). All talk of "improving society" that omits the number one improvement needed—salvation—is empty prattle.

The following passages are a list I compiled in the late 1970s. I remember the preacher, Chuck Lucas, making a comment that the Lord came to the earth to preach the message of salvation. I thought I would skim the New Testament to see if this statement was easily provable. (Boy, was it ever!) Take some time to look up these verses.

Our own convictions about sharing this salvation with others must flow from the Scriptures and from our personal relationship with Jesus himself—not from a system of external rules, requirements of leaders or a guilty conscience. Funny, isn't it, how often we share our faith so that we will feel better about ourselves? But who is the one in need—are we, or is it the individual we are reaching out to? Are we sharing our faith for his or her sake or for our own? Think about it.

- Matthew 1:21, 10:34, [18:11], 20:28, 26:28
- Mark 1:38, 2:17, 10:45
- Luke 1:47; 2:11, 30; 3:6; 4:18, 43; 5:32; 12:49; 19:10; 24:47
- John 1:29, 4:34, 5:30, 6:38, 10:10, 12:47, 14:6, 17:4, 18:37
- Acts 2:38, 3:26, 4:12, 10:43
- Romans 3:24, 5:9, 8:3, 14:9, 15:8–9
- 1 Corinthians 1:30, 6:11, 15:3
- 2 Corinthians 5:15, 21

- Galatians 1:3–4, 2:21, 3:24, 4:4–5
- Ephesians 1:7, 2:14–18, 5:25
- Philippians 2:5–11
- Colossians 1:14, 20, 22
- 1 Thessalonians 1:10, 5:9–10
- 1 Timothy 1:15, 2:5–6
- 2 Timothy 1:10
- Titus 2:14, 3:4–6
- Hebrews 1:3; 2:9, 14, 17; 5:9; 7:27; 9:15, 26, 28; 10:7; 13:12
- 1 Peter 1:18–19; 2:21, 24; 3:18
- 1 John 2:2; 3:5, 8; 4:9–10, 14
- Revelation 1:5–6

This is more than eighty passages! The implication is clear: as we follow Jesus, we will assume the same mission, the same sense of urgency.

2. Teach All Nations?

"In the King James Version, Matthew 28:19 says 'teach all nations,' whereas the New International Version reads 'make disciples of all nations.' What is the best way to teach that people need to become disciples before getting baptized if we are teaching the lost using the KJV?"

In this particular passage, the KJV is not as accurate as most modern versions. The verbs "disciple" and "teach" are closely related, but the former seldom appears in the Bible. It is understandable why the King James translators missed the nuance in Greek. Actually, the literal rendering would not be "make disciples of," but simply "disciple." At any rate, the text does not say that one must become a saved disciple before being baptized—that would be impossible since baptism is necessary for forgiveness. It strongly implies, however, that the candidate for baptism is prepared to give his life over to the Lord in discipleship. Again, while discipleship as an attitude of humble learning comes before baptism, no one "becomes a disciple" before baptism, since baptism is the final step in the transition from the world into the kingdom of Jesus—from self-will to being a disciple of Jesus.

3. 'Disciples' Only?

"We say that the proper term for a true Christian is 'disciple,' since this is the word that appears hundreds of times in the New Testament. Why don't I find the term in any of the letters, only in the Gospels and Acts?"

Good question. It is clear enough from the first five books of the New Testament that followers of Jesus are to be disciples. "Disciple" means "student." The word emphasizes that we are always learning, never perfect, in a constant state of training in the able hands of our Master. But Christians are never called disciples in the letters or Revelation. Rather, they are called "brothers and sisters," "saints," even "friends," to name a few of the many terms which designate a Christian. Why is this?

To begin with, the Gospels and Acts are written not only for members of the community of faith, but for outsiders who are still forming their impressions of Christianity. (See John 20:30–31, Luke 1:1, Acts 1:1.) To the outsider, one quite noticeable quality of a zealous follower of Jesus Christ is his or her eagerness to learn—hence the word "disciple." Yet the letters and Revelation are written to believers, to insiders, who, to one another, are best described as "brothers" or "friends."

I suggest that the term we favor probably tells us more about our own theology than about the doctrine of the Scriptures. To illustrate, if someone only used the term "brother," you would know that spiritual family relationships mean a lot to him. And if he avoids the term "disciple," perhaps the commitment of following Christ troubles him. (Maybe not.) If another person stresses that we are called to be "saints," his focus is on the holiness to which we are called, more than sheer busy-ness, commitment or activity. But then maybe he is not tied in to the fellowship, especially if he feels uncomfortable calling someone "brother."

Does the New Testament tell us to use only one word to designate a follower of Christ? Certainly not. It would probably be safest to use the whole range of appellations: brother, Christian, saint, disciple, friend, etc.

4. Discipleship and Immediate Challenge

"When we study discipleship with people, we usually challenge them to respond immediately to the call (Mark 1:16–20). But do the Gospels uniformly teach that this immediate response is normal (or normative)?"

You are right. Luke 5 shows a less than decisive Peter being called by Jesus. There are indeed differences in nuance among the four Gospels, and these should be taken into account. For example, the calling of the disciples in Mark follows the initial relationship-building phase indicated in John 1. Some months may well have gone by.

Today, we need to be sensitive to those we are studying with. There is a time for challenge, but usually it is after their own prayer and Bible study has begun to be developed. Many, if not most, people would be blown away if the first scripture we shared with them was a challenge to total commitment. For more practicals on sharing your faith, see *Shining Like Stars*. This book is replete with tips on how to study with people, how to use the Scriptures effectively and more. In all it contains some forty Bible studies you can do with your non-Christian friends.

5. Suffering

"If God is (1) perfectly loving, (2) omnipotent and (3) omniscient, why is evil so prevalent in the world? The free-will defense explains 'moral evils' such as murder and rape, yet it fails to explain 'natural evils' such as earthquakes and cancer. Is this because Satan has free will as well?"

You are right about free will being something that defines us as humans. Without the possibility of rejecting the good, we have no meaningful relationship with our Creator or with one another.

Yet disease and natural disaster appear to fall into a different category. Here are my thoughts.

I am not so sure that Satan is behind all sickness, accidents and natural disasters. Being "the evil one" is not the same as being evil. Satan is not simply the personified power of evil; he is an independent being who has chosen to rebel against God and his will.

True, everything that happens is directly caused or allowed by God to happen, but this does not mean that every time we suffer, we ought to blame it on God, any more than we should blame it on Satan.

Christians are never promised freedom from suffering. The prayer of Jabez in 1 Chronicles 4:10 is not a prayer for Christians—despite the immense popularity of religious books by that name. Bearing the cross of Jesus means that we are guaranteed suffering, and freedom from suffering is not so much a mark of spirituality as of disengagement from the fight.

Earthquakes—volcanic and tectonic activity—are essential for life on earth. They circulate the elements, bringing the heavier metals from the core and mantle to the surface. Floods make the soil fertile. Hurricanes scour the surface of the globe. These natural disasters serve as a checks-and-balances system to make our atmosphere, earth and seas beneficial. Without storms, earthquakes and floods, our planet would not be an inhabitable place at all! They are as vital for us as the 23.5-degree tilt of the earth's axis, our location 93 million miles from the sun and the moon's influence as the primary producer of tides.

The "evil," when it comes to natural ills, seems to stem from "being in the wrong place at the wrong time"—the time for a catastrophe to occur. In other words, don't build your hut on the lip of a volcano; don't build your village in the floodplain; and don't blame God if you took your chances and lost everything!

Disease accelerates the end of life. Death is not always a curse, but a blessing. Have you ever spent time with a dying man, someone in great pain? Then you know that sometimes people pray for death. Have you never prayed for the death of someone you loved? Death means an end to suffering. (Of course, as Christians we know it is not the end at all, merely a transition for us.)

As medical researchers extend our lives and reduce our levels of pain, have our relationships improved? Are we closer to God? Is this world all there is, or shouldn't we rather be preparing for the next?

Sickness demands patience and perseverance. There is no shortcut to character—Romans 5 is very clear about that. Physical and emotional pain not only toughen us up, they also help us relate to others. Empathy means every loss, pain or sickness is a hidden talent. We have something to share, something to talk about, something to use to connect through love with others. Without hardship, what heroism, courage or magnanimity of spirit would there be?

All these considerations paint a picture of a world under God's control. His providence operates through physiology, geology, psychology and whatever other "ology" there is!

For more on this subject, let me recommend C. S. Lewis' *The Problem of Pain*, Ravi Zacharias' *Deliver Us from Evil* and Philip Yancey's *What's So Amazing About Grace?*[1]

6. The Prayer of Jabez

"I noticed in one of your recent answers that you criticized the book *The Prayer of Jabez*. I felt that this book contains inaccuracies about how to become a Christian, yet the prayer does help remind us to focus on the mission of evangelizing the world. Can you please explain further why you think the prayer is unspiritual?"

Pop-Christianity seems to me to be obsessed with prosperity, receiving God's blessings and avoiding suffering. Christian bookstores carry many works which, intentionally or not, undermine God's call to sacrifice. Most people, it seems, would prefer a "crossless" Christianity. This popular volume (more than nine million sold to date) begins,

> Dear Reader, I want to teach you how to pray a daring prayer that God always answers. It is brief—only one sentence with four parts—and tucked away in the Bible, but I believe it contains the key to a life of extraordinary favor with God....

But let's focus on the prayer of Jabez itself:

> Jabez cried out to the God of Israel, "Oh, that you would bless me and enlarge my territory! Let your hand be with me, and keep me from harm so that I will be free from [or not cause] pain." And God granted his request. (1 Chronicles 4:10)

Whether God granted Jabez's request or not, what warrant do we have to assume that he will grant the same prayer on our lips? Suffering is part and parcel of the Christian life (Luke 9:23, 2 Timothy 3:12, 2 Peter 2:19–21, etc.). It is definitely a stretch to interpret "enlarging my territory" in an evangelistic sense, though the point is a good one. It is always best to use scriptures that *do* teach your point rather than ones that *don't*, or are too vague to draw a definite conclusion from!

To sum up, pain is part of life; Jesus does offer relief from much of our suffering, and yet the request for a pain-free Christian walk is unspiritual. It encourages faith in the power of prayer more than faith in the power of God. The "name it and claim it" movement (or "Word-faith," based on a misinterpretation of Mark 11) is powerful, especially in the neo-Pentecostal revival and the born-again movement at large. Interestingly, surveys consistently show that the majority of "born-again believers" in the United States do not even consider the Bible to be the absolute authority in their lives. For example, most do not accept a literal Satan and believe in relative truth ("situation ethics").

I am afraid that this book appeals most to those unwilling to shoulder the cross of Christ. Remember, it is to preach the cross that we are commissioned in the first place (1 Corinthians 1). *The Prayer of Jabez: Breaking Through to the Blessed Life* sounds too good to be true. It is.

7. All About Baptism

"I would like to know everything possible about baptism. Can you point me in the right direction?"

I am glad you want to know everything about baptism. I really want to help you. The best way, apart from your own reading of the Bible, is your own willingness to do extra study. I think if you work at it, you will find all the answers you seek.

I recommend two books: *Born of Water* and *Shining Like Stars*. These books will help you to not only answer your own questions, but also to help your friends.[2]

8. Scholars and Baptism

"My father is a denominational minister and we have disagreed over the meaning of New Testament baptism. I read in a study Bible the words of a scholar who said that the Greek indicates baptism is an 'after the fact' proclamation of one's having become a Christian. What do you think of these experts? Are they handling the Greek properly?"

To begin with, most scholars admit that the Greek allows no interpretation other than the fact that baptism was originally thought to confer forgiveness of sins. This admission includes scholars whose own denominational backgrounds discount such a view. Any scholar who dissents is not only in the minority, but is holding a position that consistently flies in the face of the linguistic and historical evidence. The fact that you came across his opinion in a study Bible should not surprise you. Of course, such additional notes are not part of the inspired text. They have been added as an aid to understanding. But that is where one can get lost—in the transition from the word of God to the word of man.

9. Origin of Baptism

"While watching the movie *Mary, Mother of Jesus* and seeing baptism depicted as sprinkling, I suddenly wondered, where did baptism come from in the first place? As I understand it, the Jewish people did not go in for baptism—or did they? The first time baptism comes up in my concordance is in Matthew 3:6. Also, where does it say in the Bible that one must be completely immersed?"

Really, these are two separate questions. Baptism "comes from" the many ablutions and washings of the OT law, although it is not urged on the people until the time of John the Baptizer. You are right: most Jewish people did not go for baptism (though some did, Luke 7:29), as it required rigorous repentance. For the same reason, most people do not go for baptism today.

As for total immersion, this is the semantic meaning of baptism. The Greek *baptisma* means immersion—nothing less—this is its definition.

10. Perfect, Up-to-Date Repentance?

"I have heard people imply that if Jesus were to come back today and we haven't repented of all sin, we won't go to heaven. However, that's not what I read in the Bible. The Bible says that the Holy Spirit is a guarantee that we're going to heaven and that we were granted forgiveness for all our sins. I thought that this was the good news! Even though we have an obligation to live according to Jesus' teachings in order to remain saved, will we be rejected from heaven if Jesus comes back before we've repented of every sin or bad attitude that we're aware of?"

I do not read this in the Word, either. Is it even possible to know of and repent of every sin we have committed? This seems to assume a lot. I would venture to say that we will never be in a state of perfection (clear conscience or not) down on this earth. Just as a father or mother is in a relationship with a child, regardless of the "goodness" of the child's performance, so too our heavenly Father is in a continual relationship with his children. Beware the destructive attitude that can bring false guilt and self-focused anxiety into our lives.

On the other hand, do not forget Psalm 101:2! As the song says, "I wanna be ready, ready when Jesus comes." Certainly, we must do all we can to walk the narrow path (Matthew 7:13–14, Luke 13:24), but I agree with you that salvation is not contingent on some state of perfection. I emphasized this point in my book, *Life to the Full*. I have often heard Hebrews 10:26 misused to imply that unless you have totally broken from your sinful habits, Jesus' blood will not cover you. This is false doctrine. (As is clear from its context, the book of Hebrews deals with those who are giving up on Jesus altogether.) Grace can always be abused—that is its nature—yet God never meant for us to remain in a perpetual state of suspense regarding our salvation.

As for the Spirit being a guarantee, yes, it is; and yet we must not "grieve" or "quench" it. A personal relationship is at stake: our relationship with God.

11. Confession of Sins

"I gather from Romans 10 (and by piecing together instances in Acts) that hearing the message, believing (and audibly confessing) Jesus as Lord, repenting of sins and being baptized are necessary for salvation. But why do people have to confess their sins before being baptized? I realize it's not wrong, but why insist on it? I cannot find anywhere in the New Testament mandating this practice. In Matthew 3:6 people were confessing their sins, since this was a baptism of repentance (Mark 1:4), but Paul differentiates the two

baptisms in Acts 19:4. The sorcerers in Ephesus also confessed their sins (Acts 19:18), but they were already believers.
I just want to make sure we're not adding a tradition of men
to God's requirements for baptism."

You make a good case. I myself see no passage in the New
Testament requiring people to confess all their sins to
another human being. James 5:16 is for those who are
already believers. The passages on John's baptism establish
the precedent of confession before baptism, yet they do not
establish a command for us. And while I consistently try to
get the men I am studying the Scriptures with to "come
clean," acknowledging their sins with some degree of specificity, this custom is more for their benefit—to create a spirit
of openness and facilitate future help when needed—than
for the sake of obedience to a Biblical command. I make it
a habit of confessing my sins to them, as well.

Sometimes it is taught that repentance is defective if all sins
are not confessed. I for one (speaking personally, not for all
my fellow leaders) have several problems with this teaching.

As the years go by, we become aware of more and
more sins in our lives. To some extent, sensitivity to sin is
a function of spiritual maturity—as opposed to repentance. Some people, in fact, are "re-baptized" every few
years, as their awareness of sin increases. As a good friend
put it, "It is always easier to doubt your baptism than to
trust in the grace of God."

The lack of crystal clear Biblical teaching, such as we
have in the case of the requirement of faith, repentance,
and baptism, should make us wary of amplifying God's
requirements—even though our intentions are good.

We do not see this custom in practice in the book of
Acts, which records how the early church understood
apostolic teaching.

Some people have been so deeply traumatized (sexual
abuse, psychological torment, etc.) that they seem incapable of total "openness" until they have been disciples for
a few years. It takes time to build trust, and deep, intimate

secrets do not readily give themselves up to persons who are still relatively new acquaintances. This is not to say we must stop preaching the need to be open and honest, only that we must be careful not to require more of a penitent person than God himself requires.

12. God and Satan

"When I was studying literature at university, I came across writers like Lewis Carroll who, in his book *Alice in Wonderland,* depicts our life as a chess game between our Creator and our adversary, and we humans are their pawns. Is this the case? It seems that Satan must have challenged God's verdict in regard to his sentence to eternal condemnation. To satisfy him, God has allowed him to test and delude man, and to prove to him that God's created beings can choose to obey and trust him, though they are much less than he. It seemed like a deal Lucifer made with God. But with that pact come also the horrific events of humanity, including World Wars I and II and the Holocaust. Am I right in saying so? What's your view on all this?"

I think the way you put it is very close to the truth, except the part about reigning in hell or "eternal condemnation"—this is more of a concept of the Catholic Church or John Milton. When Satan goes into hell, he will be burned up, as the depiction in Revelation suggests. But, yes, God is demonstrating to his one-time friend the superiority of his system. And a regrettable result of free will—the alternative to coercion—is evil.

13. Transubstantiation

"Could you shed some light on the Roman Catholic interpretation of the Lord's Supper? A Catholic friend of mine believes strongly that they eat and drink the actual flesh and blood of Jesus."

Today I visited the Catholic shrine of the Virgin Mary of Guadalupe in Mexico City. The "Mass" is frequently

offered. Mass entails transubstantiation, the literal sacrifice
of the body and blood of Christ in the form of the communion wafer and the wine. The "sacrifice" is offered by
"priests." Yet the New Testament says that Jesus cannot be
sacrificed again; his death was "once for all" (Hebrews
9:12, 26; 10:10). Moreover, in the New Testament there are
no special priests. The unbiblical rise of the priesthood
through the generations following the first century is well
documented.

Simply put, Catholics believe that communion, or the
Eucharist, is a re-presentation of the sacrifice of Christ,
whereas the Protestant position is that it is only a representation. When Jesus said during the Last Supper, "This is
my body," it is hard to believe that he meant he had two
bodies—the one doing the talking, as well as the bread
they were about to eat. To claim that the bread is mysti-
cally transformed inwardly, though not outwardly, into the
body of Christ, requires an illogical and unwarranted leap
of faith!

14. Once Saved, Always Saved?

"What is your best answer to counter the 'Once Saved,
Always Saved' argument?"

There are literally hundreds of scriptures which demolish
the claim that it is impossible, once one has come to know
Jesus Christ, to lose one's salvation. The answer to the
question of "once saved, always saved" is a useful study in
its own right, not just a response to common false doctrine.[3] Consider the following verses:

Hebrews 10:26–31
It is possible, through deliberately rejecting the sacrifice
of Christ, to lose our salvation. Though the passage is
emphatically clear, some insist it applies only to non-
Christians or to unsaved churchgoers. But verse 29 ("the
blood of the covenant that sanctified him") and verse 30
("The Lord will judge *his* people") show that the writer has
in mind the covenant people—people already saved.

Hebrews 6:4–6

It is impossible to bring certain people back to repentance: those who have passed the point of no return or who have "fallen away." The phrase "crucifying the Son of God all over again" strongly implies that they have already shared in Jesus' death and resurrection. (Hebrews 6:8–9 continues the thought.) Other verses in Hebrews to consider: 2:1–3; 3:12–14; 4:1, 11; 6:11–12; 10:36; 12:14–15 and 13:4.

Romans 8:28–39

Nothing can separate us from the love of God, but it is *our* responsibility to keep ourselves in God's love (Jude 21). We have free will; many advocates of "once saved, always saved" deny this.

John 10:28–29

Although this passage is often cited as proof of the impossibility of apostasy (falling away or losing one's salvation), it does not rule out turning one's back on God. (See Luke 9:62.) It is only impossible for external powers to drag away a disciple *against his or her will.*

2 Peter 2:20–22

This passage clinches the argument. These people have "escaped the corruption of the world," which is possible only by participating in the divine nature (2 Peter 1:4). The corruption of the world is vividly symbolized by vomit and mud. It is tortuous to argue that the "washing" applies to a non-Christian.

The Real Issue

At first glance, the topic of falling away appears to be a doctrinal subject. In fact, it strikes directly at the heart of the issue: commitment. Read together, these verses are quite challenging to us all!

15. Philemon 1:6

'Greetings from the Ukraine! In Philemon 1:6, Paul and Timothy ask Philemon to be 'active in sharing [his] faith.'

That's the scripture that we use to teach others about our mission in the world. Yet, in the Russian translations (especially the Modern Translation) we have a different connotation of the scripture. There it talks about the fact that 'sharing your faith actively' (it nearly says 'with other Christians') is designed to benefit you spiritually. Thus, 'sharing your faith' here means openness with disciples and developing deep spiritual relationships with them. What do you know about what Paul and Timothy really meant by this verse?"

You are quite right. Apart from the NIV, virtually no translation takes verse 6 as a passage on evangelism. It does not fit the passage, the context or the Greek. There are *plenty* of verses on evangelism in the New Testament, and I am sure you know a load of them! But we should avoid making passages say what they do not say. Many Bible readers limit themselves by reading only one translation.

The word translated "sharing" or fellowship is the Greek *koinonia,* a term usually associated with life in the church family. My Russian Bible reads *obsheniye* (did I get that right?), which is the literal translation of *koinonia,* while the Ukrainian *slisnist* (did I butcher it?) presumably means exactly the same.

In the specific passage, Paul is encouraging Philemon to deepen his fellowship—as he has done in the past—and to transform the fellowship of the local church by granting the slave Onesimus his freedom.

Finally, let's consider how some of the other *English* versions translate Philemon 6, emphasis is mine.

> I pray that the *fellowship* of your faith may become effective through the knowledge of every good thing which is in you for Christ's sake. (NAS)
>
> I pray that the *sharing* of your faith may promote the knowledge of all the good that is ours in Christ. (RSV)
>
> I pray that your *fellowship* in faith may come to expression in full knowledge of all the good we can do for Christ. (NJB)

16. Restoration

"I have a question about restorations. I am helping a sister to return to the church and am uncertain as to whether my friend is still in the darkness. She has been coming to services, having quiet times, and dealing with the issues that caused her to leave in the first place. She claims that she is in the light again, and I cannot find any scriptures to share with her that would show that she is in the dark until the day we take her good confession in front of the church. How do we know when someone is officially 'restored'?"

Biblically, "restoration" is something we all need, whenever we are wilting (Psalm 23:1–3) or caught in a sin (Galatians 6:1). I have no desire to argue about words, but when someone wanders away from the flock (James 5:19), and then returns, I think "restoration" is a misnomer. This is because "restoration" is something for those who are saved, not for those who are lost.

Now, as to when exactly someone who gives up on the life of discipleship is lost, I do not wish to hazard a guess. God knows. Yet God's word states that those who continue to live the worldly lifestyle will not make it (Galatians 5:19–21). For how long he or she can "fall away," I cannot say either. All of us have bad moments. For example, if someone, in a crisis of faith, attends church Sunday, "quits" on Monday, and returns Tuesday—before the Wednesday midweek service—was that person lost for a day? How we answer this question probably says more about our understanding of God than about the true status of the individual who is struggling, since we do not know the heart as well as Jesus Christ does. Yes, I am aware that people's words give us a good clue as to what's inside, as Luke 6:45 says; but still, I think that we need to be careful about judging people's hearts, thoughts and attitudes, which is best left to God (Hebrews 4:12–13). For example, I don't know how much arsenic I can have in my bloodstream before I will actually die, but this uncertainty does not make me want to drink arsenic in small doses!

Finally, I hope you will be able to read what I have written in the appendix of my book *Shining Like Stars* on restorations. My view is that it will be very hard to prove Biblically that someone who has already come back to the fold is still in the darkness. I hope you don't mind this little "homework assignment."

Notes

[1] C. S. Lewis, *The Problem of Pain* (New York: The Macmillan Co., 1944). Ravi Zacharias, *Deliver Us from Evil: Restoring the Soul in a Disintegrating Culture* (Dallas: Word Publishing, 1996). Philip Yancey, *What's So Amazing About Grace?* (Grand Rapids: Zondervan, 1997).

[2] For bibliography information for these books and others commonly used throughout the chapters, see the Abbreviations page at the beginning of this book.

[3] This brief study is updated from material that I wrote in 1986. I have included more on this issue in the chapter "Advanced Guard the Gospel" in *Shining Like Stars*.

2
Difficult Passages

1. *Leviticus 10*

"In Leviticus 10 Nadab and Abihu were struck down for getting the incense recipe wrong. Isn't this a bit severe?"

God had already indicated that he would not tolerate improvising when it came to offering the sacred fire (Exodus 30). It seems these sons of Aaron got into trouble because of the state in which they approached their priestly duties, as recorded in Leviticus 10:9: "You [Aaron] and your sons are not to drink wine or other fermented drink whenever you go into the Tent of Meeting, or you will die." It appears the fatal carelessness of Nadab and Abihu sprang from their inebriated condition.

2. *Circle of the Earth*

"I have heard it taught that Isaiah 40 proves that the earth is round. What are your thoughts on this?"

It is true that the verse portrays the earth as round, yet what does "round" mean? Turning to the text, we read:

> He sits enthroned above the circle of the earth,
>   and its people are like grasshoppers.
> He stretches out the heavens like a canopy,
>   and spreads them out like a tent to live in.
> (Isaiah 40:22)

The earth, in poetic language, is described as a "circle." A circle is two-dimensional, and unless rotated about an axis, it is actually flat. Moreover, the heavens are described as being "stretched out" like a canopy. The ancients often conceived of the earth as a disk covered by a semispherical vault. This passage appears to reflect that understanding. It should not be pressed to yield "scientific insight" into the shape of our planet.

In other words, this passage (and others like it) was never intended to comment on the dimensions or shape of the earth, any more than the Bible's speaking of "sunrise" and "sunset" was meant to impart the old Ptolemaic geocentric dogma. Poetry normally paints a picture; there are subjective elements which, left where they are, convey truth. Yet if they are wrested from their literary context, a distorted picture may emerge.

3. Did Jacob See God?

"In Genesis 32:22–30, after his wrestling match, Jacob says, 'I saw God face to face, and yet my life was spared.' But 1 John 4:12 says 'No one has ever seen God.' Did Jacob see God?"

You have said it yourself: Jacob did not see God—at least not fully! No sinful man can see God in his full glory and purity and brilliance without being vaporized. That is my take on Habakkuk 1:13: "Your [God's] eyes are too pure to look on evil; you [God] cannot tolerate wrong." Yet Jacob did see God—in some sense. He "saw" that no one, by sheer grit, will and perseverance, can back God into a corner, force his hand or extract blessings. He "saw" his own weakness and felt it painfully. Therefore, it all depends on how you define the word "see."

Only in Jesus do we really see God (John 1:14, 18; 14:9). Yet when we look at Jesus, we are not being exposed to the complete, intense, terrifying, awesome, overwhelming presence of God. Even to catch a sideward glimpse of him is suffocating, enervating, totally debilitating (Daniel 10:17). No one has ever seen him in one sense, but we all see him in another. So the answer remains, without any intention of double talk, both *yes* and *no*.

4. Face to Face?

"Exodus 33:11 says the LORD spoke to Moses face to face, yet in 33:20 God says Moses cannot see his face, as no one may see him and live. Isn't this a contradiction? Please explain."

Yes, it is a contradiction. On the surface, anyway. But surface contradictions are not the same thing as true contradictions. The problem in this case arises because often when the Bible describes God's interaction with man, it does so anthropomorphically. That is, it describes things in human terms (*anthropos* is Greek for "human being"). Exodus 33 (see also Number 12) says that Moses enjoyed a special relationship with the Lord.

In Exodus 33:11, "face to face" is a figure of speech; it emphasizes the intimacy of Moses' relationship with God. In 33:20, however, "face" is referring to a full encounter with the Lord's presence—the overwhelming power and intensity of encountering the living God. This is what the apostle John is alluding to in John 1:18.

5. 'Saved Through Childbirth'

"What did Paul mean when he wrote, 'Women will be saved through childbirth'?"

For the modern reader, 1 Timothy 2:15 is certainly a strange passage. Certainly Paul is not saying that a woman can live a godless life and automatically go to heaven—as long as she has children! So what is he saying?

It is essential to know something about the false teachings Paul is addressing in 1 Timothy. He is instructing the evangelist Timothy to combat a form of Gnosticism, from the Greek word *gnosis*, meaning "knowledge." Gnostics taught that the body was evil and sex was a necessary evil. Many advocated celibacy, forbade marriage and prohibited the consumption of various foods (1 Timothy 4:1–5). Whereas the Gnostics thought that childbirth was somehow unrighteous, as it necessitated intercourse, Paul insists that women who have children will indeed be saved—provided, of course, they live the right sort of life.

With knowledge of its historical and theological context, this otherwise obscure passage makes sense. While all the basic teachings of the Bible are fairly easy to grasp without a lot of background knowledge, this does not mean that every verse in the Scriptures is easy to understand (2 Peter 3:15–16) without an appreciation for the cultural context and setting.

6. Saul's Death

"The accounts of Saul's death recorded in 2 Samuel 1:1–16 and in 1 Chronicles 10:1–5 seem to contradict each other. Is there an explanation for these two different accounts of the same event?"

The account of Saul's death in 1 Chronicles 10 mirrors the account of 1 Samuel 31, the chapter immediately preceding 2 Samuel 1. In the narrative, we see that Saul took his own life, whereas the Amalekite claims to have killed Saul himself. (An "assisted suicide"?) For his audacity, the Amalekite loses his life. But was he telling the truth, or simply hoping for some reward, some "bounty money"? As the Bible twice relates that Saul fell on his own sword, and his armor-bearer did the same, there is no corroborating witness for the Amalekite's version of what happened. My conclusion: he was lying. (And David judges him by his own words.)

7. Mark 16

"I have understood that the passing on of the gifts of the Holy Spirit came through the apostles, but I am hoping you can shed light on the laying on of hands mentioned in Mark 16:15–18. This scripture says, among other things, that those who believe will be able to 'place their hands on sick people, and they will get well' (NIV), and 'they will lay their hands on the sick, and they will recover' (RSV). I have searched a few commentaries and have not come up with a conclusive answer. Your help would be greatly appreciated."

The prediction Jesus made in Mark 16 was fulfilled in the book of Acts. The final verse or two of Mark's gospel state that the Lord went with the disciples and confirmed his word (past tense) through the miracles they did. It is hard to prove the "charismatic" (neo-Pentecostal) position: that Jesus was describing actions that should characterize all Christians in future generations.

I believe the key is found in verse 20, which mentions the purpose of these miracles: to confirm the spoken word of God. Never in the Bible do we read of the written word being confirmed miraculously. In other words, once the word was committed to writing—once it had become *Scripture*—no miracles were needed. Since we have the entire faith in scriptural form in the New Testament (Jude 3), we do not need miracles, as did the first generation of Christianity. This is not to say God cannot or no longer does perform miracles, only that conditions are quite different today. Mark 16 has a specific church historical context, and without awareness of the distinctions I am describing, it is easy to misapply what Jesus spoke about.

For other thoughts, see my book *The Spirit*.

8. Kingdom of God Vs. Kingdom of Heaven

"In Matthew 11:11–12, a reference to the 'kingdom of heaven' is made. Several other NT passages refer to the 'kingdom of God.' Is there a distinction between the two?"

Since Matthew is writing for an audience that is predominantly Jewish, he prefers to use the phrase "kingdom of heaven"—unlike Mark and Luke. Jews often avoided saying the actual word "God," out of reverence. So there is really no difference at all between the two phrases. In either case, the king who rules the kingdom is Lord.

9. Armageddon

"What exactly is the battle of Armageddon? Is there going to be a literal battle, as Revelation 16 seems to indicate? And how can we prepare for this awful battle at the end of time?"

To begin with, the battle of Armageddon—Armageddon comes from the Hebrew har-Megiddo, hill/mountain of Megiddo—is not necessarily a literal battle. Revelation is a book rich with symbolism, including some 500 allusions to the Old Testament. The general environs of Megiddo were a frequent battleground. What did Revelation 16:16 conjure up in the mind of the reader or listener familiar with OT history? Warfare. A showdown. I personally do not view "Armageddon" in any literal sense, though it is true that one of the central messages of Revelation is that the forces of good will ultimately triumph over the forces of evil. There are many obstacles to taking the language of Revelation literally; I am afraid the preachers on pop religious radio are misleading many.

The earliest recorded "battle of Armageddon" took place nearly 4400 years ago, and there have been dozens—perhaps scores—of battles in the region of Megiddo since that time. In other words, "Armageddon" is an image of warfare, for it reminds us of the battles waged by men of God from time immemorial. (As you will see in the following table, there have been a good number of battles waged there by pagans as well.)

If this is not a literal battle, there is no way to prepare for it physically. And yet both testaments urge us always to be ready to meet God. Rather than stockpiling water, canned goods and ammunition—as some survivalist groups practice—it is the Lord's will that we heap up righteousness and good deeds, sharing what we have (not hoarding it) with as many as possible.

If you are like me, you will be amazed at the sheer number of battles that have been waged in close proximity to the hill of Megiddo. Following is a table of those battles that history has seen fit to record for us.

As we have seen, by the time the Lord employed the Armageddon metaphor through John in the book of Revelation, at least a dozen battles had been fought in the area of Megiddo. An apt picture of the cosmic battle between God and Satan indeed! God's word assures us, in

Battles at Meggido[1]

Year	Battle	Location
2350 BC	Pepi I and the "Gazelle's Head"	Jezreel Valley
1479 BC	Thutmose III v. Canaanites	Megiddo
1430 BC	Amenhotep II in the Valley	Jezreel Valley
1360–1350 BC	Biridiya v. Labayu	Megiddo
1125 BC	Deborah and Barak v. Sisera	Taanach and Mount Tabor
1090 BC	Gideon v. Midianites/Amalekites	Hill of Moreh/Endor
1016 BC	Saul and Jonathan v. Philistines	Mount Gilboa
925 BC	Shosenq I (Shishak) at Megiddo	Megiddo
841 BC	Jehu v. Joram and Ahaziah	Jezreel
609 BC	Necho II v. Josiah	Megiddo
218 BC	Antiochus III v. Ptolemy IV	Mount Tabor
55 BC	Gabinius v. Alexander	Mount Tabor
67 AD	Vespasian v. Jewish Rebels	Mount Tabor
940 AD	Ikhshidids v. Abbasids	Lejjun
946 AD	Ikhshidids v. Hamdanids	Lejjun/Aksal
975 AD	Byzantines v. Fatimids	Mount Tabor
1113 AD	Maudud v. Crusaders	Mount Tabor
1182 AD	Saladin v. Daburiyans	Daburiya
1182 AD	Saladin v. Crusaders	Forbelet
1183 AD	Saladin v. Crusaders	'Ayn Jalut
1187 AD	Saladin v. Crusaders	Mount Tabor, etc.
1217 AD	Fifth Crusade v. Muslims	Mount Tabor
1247 AD	Ayyubids v. Crusaders	Mount Tabor
1260 AD	Mamlukes v. Mongols	'Ayn Jalut
1263 AD	Mamlukes v. Hospitallers	Mount Tabor
1264 AD	Hospitallers/Templars v. Mamlukes	Lejjun
1735 AD	Zahir al-'Umar v. Nablus-Saqr Alliance	al-Rawdah
1771–73 AD	Zahir al-'Umar at Lejjun	Lejjun
1799 AD	Napoleon v. Ottomans	Mount Tabor
1918 AD	Allenby v. Ottomans	Megiddo
1948 AD	Israelis v. Arabs	Mishmar Haemek
1948 AD	Israelis v. Arabs	Zarin, Megiddo and Lejjun
1967 AD	Israelis v. Arabs	Ramat David Airfield
1973 AD	Israelis v. Syrians	Ramat David Airfield

the book of Revelation, that ultimately he will vanquish every cause that sets itself up against him, his Son and his kingdom. In order to walk the walk of disciples, we need this assurance.

10. Matthew 28— A Late Addition?

"I recently read that there is much criticism among Biblical scholars as to the authenticity of the Great Commission passage. It is alleged that Matthew 28:18–20 is unauthentic, a product of second generation Christianity, reflecting a theology characteristic of the end of that generation rather than its beginning. Why do many scholars believe this statement?"

An academic question requires an academic answer. I think probably the book you are reading is itself at least a generation or two old. Yes, it used to be more fashionable to assign late dates to the books of the New Testament, and to parts of these books, like the Great Commission section of Matthew, but this is no longer so much in vogue.

The words "I am with you always" suggest the world might *not* end in the first generation. This is significant because scholars used to believe all early Christians expected an imminent end of the world. While the New Testament does exhort us to be ready, I have difficulty developing such a concrete doctrine from the pages of the New Testament. Clearly some people expected it, others did not, and many simply did not say. It was difficult for NT scholars to believe that Jesus or the early church could have conceived of the world continuing for generations beyond their own time. And yet there are many hints in the New Testament. For example, Ephesians 3:21 speaks of "glory in the church...throughout all generations."

Scholars sometimes point to the Trinitarian formula (Father, Son, Holy Spirit) as a later liturgical development. And yet the trinity appears many times in the New

Testament—though never explicitly designated "the Trinity"—not even here. Admittedly, the wording is different from what we read in Acts 2:38, "in the name of Jesus Christ." On the other hand, the Lord never told us to utter certain words—a baptismal formula—when we immerse those we evangelize. The Trinitarian formula may have a second or third generation feel to it, but that does not disqualify it as being authentic or true to the original words Jesus spoke on the mountain in Galilee.

At any rate, I think nearly all conservative scholars accept the ending of Matthew as original. It is not a "late addition." It certainly does not reflect the gentler times of a church settling down and making peace with the world, for it is her charter, her "mission statement," her marching orders. And the battle for the world is still being waged.

11. Chronology

"Were two different chronological systems in use? John 19:13–14a reads, 'When Pilate heard this, he brought Jesus out and sat down on the judge's seat at a place known as the Stone Pavement (which in Aramaic is *Gabbatha*). It was the day of Preparation of Passover Week, about the sixth hour.' Yet Matthew 27:45 reads 'From the sixth hour until the ninth hour darkness came over all the land.' How can Jesus be before Pilate and on the cross?"

Yes indeed, we are dealing with different chronological systems. The time system of John is different from what we find in the other three Gospels. Of course Jesus can't be simultaneously before Pilate and on the cross. Competing and sometimes conflicting time systems are found throughout both testaments. In the Old Testament, for example, the religious year starts in the spring, based on the Exodus. But the legal year starts in the autumn, and Jews even today celebrate Rosh Hashanah (new year) around September. But the solar year begins in early winter.

In the case you are writing about, Matthew follows the Jewish system. The first hour is at sunrise, making the sixth hour noon. (See also Matthew 20:5.) In John, the sixth hour is 6:00 AM, since the Roman system ran midnight to midnight. In John 1:39 we read that Jesus met his future disciples at about the tenth hour, and they spent the day together. It would be odd if this were the tenth hour in Matthew's system—4:00 PM! But it makes perfect sense if this is the late morning, around 10:00 AM. In John 4:6, Jesus sits down at Jacob's well on the sixth hour. With two twelve-hour cycles in the day, this would be 6:00 PM, a typical time for watering livestock and preparing to eat. The middle of the day (noon or the sixth hour by Matthew's system) would be fiercely hot and not the time to draw water.

To sum up, the Synoptic Gospels (Matthew, Mark and Luke) follow the Jewish system. John—different from these three Gospels in many respects, including timekeeping—follows the Roman system. Therefore, there is no contradiction.

12. Was Paul Inspired?

"Paul says in 1 Corinthians 7:12 that certain instructions are from him, not from God. How does this fit in with the entire Bible being God-breathed?"

In 1 Corinthians 7 Paul was reminding the Corinthians of what Jesus had already revealed on the subject of marriage ("not I, but the Lord"). Yet Jesus never gave direct, specific advice on marriages between Christians and non-Christians. This is why Paul says "I, not the Lord." He is certainly not denying his own inspiration as an apostle.

13. Interpretation

"I have been reading the book *Is There a God?* by John Oakes. I have found this book most interesting, but there is one question that still bothers me about the creation account. I do not have a problem with believing the theory that the earth is very old, but isn't it wrong to interpret the Bible in order to try to make it reasonable to man when

man is not like God? Surely we can only think on a humanistic level and isn't God's way of doing things totally beyond
the thought processes of man—even scientists? I would
appreciate your views on this as it concerns me greatly."

Certainly I agree with you that we ought not to force God's
word into a comfortable, humanistic mold which com-
mends itself to our reasoning, flatters our egos or makes for
a suave interpretation. This would be totally wrong. And
yes, God is infinitely far above us—Isaiah 55:8–9.

We are under no obligation to tone down God's word
or to make it appear politically correct. As for the ancient-
earth idea (which I accept, as you may have read in my
book on Genesis, *The God Who Dared*), I believe we need
to accept nature/science as one channel through which
God reveals himself. This is what Romans 1:20 actually
says. His word is another channel, in fact the primary one.
Since God will not contradict himself, a contradiction
between science and theology means either wrong science
or wrong theology.

We must take our interpretative cues from God's word
itself, where they exist. We need to work hard to become
the best possible exegetes we can. I always recommend
the excellent book by Gordon Fee and Douglas Stuart,
How to Read the Bible for All Its Worth. As we approach
any Biblical passage, we must work hard to "rightly
divide" (2 Timothy 2:15 KJV). The Word doesn't always do
this for us. We have to work at it, think it over (2 Timothy 2:7)
and realize that a good many passages are far from obvious
as to their meaning (2 Peter 3:15–16).

In other words, *all* of us need to interpret. God's word
commands us to meditate, think over, explore and wrestle
with the Scriptures. Since none of us is an infallible Bible
student, we are left no other choice. If we claim to have
"arrived"—as a movement or as individuals—we will cease
to responsibly study the Bible. At this point, we will have
lost our ability to distinguish truth from error. This is a
challenge to all our readers: Work hard at your Bible

study. For all of us individually, and all of us together as God's church, will be judged by it!

14. Outsiders

"In Luke 9:49–50 some of the apostles tell Jesus they tried to stop someone who was driving out demons in his name, yet Jesus told them not to stop the man because, 'Whoever is not against you is for you.' Where do we draw the line between disputable matters (Romans 14:1) and refuting false doctrine in other religious groups? If I meet someone who by my best reckoning has a saved relationship with God, should I follow Jesus' advice in Luke 9 ('Do not stop them...')?"

As for the exorcist of Luke 9, here was a man who was, in all likelihood, right with God under the old covenant. In time he would likely hook up with the Jesus movement. He already recognized the power of Jesus' name. We simply do not have any other information about him—not enough to be dogmatic. (But remember, driving out demons does not necessarily mean someone is saved, as we see in Matthew 7:22, Acts 19:13 and other passages.)

You are right that there are both matters of opinion and central Biblical doctrines—which do not fall into the opinion category, but are matters of truth on which there can be no compromise (1 Timothy 1:3). Surely our thrust as a movement must be *positive*—the proclamation of the gospel—more than *negative*—criticizing others. In principle, anyone who holds to the Word and teaches others to do the same is right with God (John 8:31), yet as we all know, it is a "narrow road" (Matthew 7:13–14).

The modern, politically correct spirit of nonjudgmentalism can be taken too far. Two non-negotiable issues which separate true disciples from all others are (1) conversion and (2) commitment. Has the person truly obeyed the gospel (2 Thessalonians 1:8), doing what the apostles taught was necessary for salvation? And having believed, repented and been baptized, does he or she now hold to the teaching (Acts 2:42) and call others to do the same? (Colossians 1:18–2:1). There are groups that teach the truth about conversion but are far from the spirit of Christ when it comes to their commitment. And there are others who are highly devoted, yet live in error concerning the basics of the gospel. We must watch both our life and our doctrine (1 Timothy 4:16).

In my experience, committed members of various religious groups, when taught the way of God more accurately, are eager to join with the movement of disciples—and many have done so. So keep preaching the Word, and let God change people's hearts and convict them of the truth.

The more you share your own faith, the more you will cherish God's grace; appreciate the narrowness of the road we walk; understand how far from the truth most religious groups have drifted; and be able to walk the sometimes fine line between "disputable matters" (Romans 14:1) and the first principles of the gospel. Let us follow the wise direction of Rupertus Meldenius:[2]

> In essentials, unity;
> in non-essentials, liberty;
> in all things, charity.

15. Record of Wrongs?

"Genesis 18:20 says that God wanted to go to Sodom and Gomorrah to see if what they had done was as bad as the outcry against them. But I thought that God is all knowing. Also, Revelation 20:12 mentions 'the books' in which our deeds are written. But again, if God is all knowing, what is the purpose of a written record?"

All of this is for our benefit. The Bible is written so that we humans can understand it, relate to it. God is totally above us, beyond us, greater than us. Read Isaiah 55:8–9, John 1:18 and scores of other passages that stress how absolutely different from us the Almighty is. Accordingly, God bends himself to our language, to our very modes of thinking and speaking. This is called "anthropomorphism"—putting things in human terms. We frequently read of God's "hand" or his "eyes." We find him "repenting," and we find him "moving"—whereas in fact the Word teaches he is everywhere at all times. The Bible is written for us.

The visit to Sodom was for Abraham's sake, not because God lacked "intelligence." The image of the book—the "record of wrongs"—signifies that nothing will be hidden from the Lord. Ultimately, all of us will give an account of ourselves.

God knows all, needs nothing and is infinitely above our world. Yet he chooses to allow us to live, move and have our being in him. And he speaks to us, not in the language of physics, metaphysics and eternity, but in words and idioms comprehensible to every man and woman.

16. Death and Hades

"In Revelation 20:13 it says that 'death and Hades gave up the dead that were in them.' What exactly is meant by 'death and Hades'? I always thought that Hades was part of a Greek myth, so why is it in the Bible?"

Hades is the Greek god of the underworld, yes, but Hades has another meaning: the underworld itself. Tartarus is the section of Hades where the evil angels—and probably also unsaved humans—are kept (2 Peter 2:4). Paradise is the other part of Hades, where the saved enter after death, before the Lord's return to take us to be with him in heaven (John 14:3).

Death and Hades appear to be virtual synonyms in Revelation 20:13. No longer will death have power over anyone; no longer will the abode of the dead be able to contain them, as it is time for all to face judgment.

17. 'Perfection' in 1 Corinthians 13

"Is 'perfection' in 1 Corinthians 13 referring to the canonization of the New Testament? I have heard that 'perfection' is neuter in the Greek, and so cannot refer to Jesus'
coming again—otherwise it would be masculine. But
could it refer to heaven?"

Here is what I usually say about 1 Corinthians 13 (in addition to my comments in my book *The Spirit* in the chapter
covering 1 Corinthians 12–14).

The passage is susceptible to more than one interpretation. At any rate, it's not the clearest text when it comes
to demonstrating the presence or absence of the miraculous gifts of the Holy Spirit today. I encourage people not
to rely on it for a definitive interpretation of this matter.

The arguments based on the gender of the perfect in
Greek are weak at best and in my view suspect. This I discuss in *The Spirit*.

The purpose of the miraculous gifts needs examining.
This takes up a whole chapter in *The Spirit*. It does relate
to the formation of the NT canon, along with the laying of
the apostolic foundation for the early church. Ephesians
2:20 has the NT prophets at the foundation level of the
church—done, laid, not needed now. If there are
prophets, then there would be apostles too.

To return to 1 Corinthians 13, knowing fully or in part
has to do *not* with omniscience, but with completeness of
God's revelation. The Bible nowhere guarantees we will
have all knowledge in heaven, for God alone is omniscient. Paul's argument seems to be that when we know
fully, there will no longer be any need for prophecy.
Prophecy was a necessary filler during the time most
churches had only a few NT documents, and the apostles
could not be everywhere at once, in person or in letter.

I am extremely reluctant to challenge people's experiences directly. ("You didn't see a healing; it was fake!")
Only after I have laid a solid basis for future discussion by

nailing down discipleship do I dare to challenge the validity of experiences—I keep returning to, hammering, encouraging, reminding them of their commitment to the Word. On "tongues," I take a more direct approach, though, as the New Testament teaches that they are human languages (Acts 2 onward). I have heard religious people speaking in "tongues" many times, yet never had any reason to believe these were authentic miracles.

18. Luke 22:15–18

"My flatmate and I were discussing Luke 22:15–18, where Jesus says that he will not 'eat it again until it finds fulfillment in the kingdom of God' or drink again 'until the kingdom of God comes.' In verse 16, does the word 'it' refer to the Passover, and so is Jesus saying the Passover is complete when the kingdom of God is fulfilled? If so, is this a reference to his eating with his disciples after the resurrection? Or is Jesus referring to a time after Pentecost or even after Judgment Day? It seemed to us that the day of Pentecost would be the more obvious answer, but Matthew 26:29 reads, '...I drink it anew with you in my Father's kingdom.' (Heaven?) This knocked us for a six."[3]

Since the New Testament teaches that the communion meal is not just a fellowship with our brothers and sisters in Christ, but also with Christ himself ("This is my body"), it seems most reasonable to consider the Lord's Supper as the event in which the fulfillment mentioned takes place. As far as we know, the disciples first observed the Lord's Supper in obedience to Jesus' instructions (in all four Gospels, as well as the account in 1 Corinthians 11) after Pentecost. The kingdom in this passage is not heaven, but the church on earth.

As you notice, how you define "kingdom" has quite a bearing on how you interpret a passage. "Kingdom" may refer to heaven (2 Timothy 4:18), the will of God (Matthew 6:9), God's rule over the entire earth (as in the Psalms), the kingdom of Israel (Matthew 21:43), or the church itself

(Revelation 5:10). Furthermore, the Bible often speaks of the kingdom "coming" whenever the King "comes"—whether bringing reward or punishment—and we witness such "comings" in a number of verses in both testaments. (See, for example, Isaiah 19:1.)

In Luke 22 Jesus anticipates a time when he will again join his disciples in a fellowship meal. But before that could happen, he needed to fulfill his work of redemption and ascend to heaven. There, crowned King, he would reign over the kingdom of light, which all the saints enjoy (Colossians 1:6, 10–12).

19. Martyrdom of Zechariah

"In Matthew 23:35 Jesus mentioned the blood of Zechariah son of Berekiah, seeming to point to the prophet mentioned in the last book of the Hebrew Bible (Chronicles). But Jesus refers to this Zechariah as the son of Jehoiada, not Berekiah. Zechariah son of Berekiah is one of the postexilic prophets. And does the choice of this Zechariah have anything to do with the blood of Abel?"

Critics (and most Biblical scholars) claim that Jesus was mistaken about Zechariah's father's name. He must mean the son of Jehoiada, who was killed in the temple. And yet several considerations must be taken into account:

- There are several Zechariahs in the Old Testament.
- There were a number of men killed near the altar of the temple.
- Zechariah the son of Jehoiada, though mentioned in 2 Chronicles 24:22 (the last book of the Old Testament in the order of the Hebrew Bible), is not the last Zechariah chronologically. Surely if Jesus is making a sweeping statement, the span would more likely be from Abel (the earliest OT martyr) to Zechariah (one of the final figures of the Old Testament, around 500 BC), not from Abel to the son of Jehoiada (eighth

century BC). If Esther had been executed—fortunately she was not—she might have been the final martyr of OT times (400s BC). Or if Jesus was including the intertestamental period, the martyrs of the second century bc would have made a good reference.

- There are other executions referred to by the New Testament (e.g., see Hebrews 11) which are not recorded in the Old Testament, yet this does not mean they never took place.

No, Jesus did not get his facts wrong, nor did Matthew put erroneous words into Jesus' mouth. Zechariah is linked with Abel because they represent the righteous persecuted of the Old Testament, appearing at the beginning and the end chronologically. This is the link between Abel and Zechariah.

Finally, two helpful reference books in resolving Bible difficulties are Gleason Archer's *An Encyclopedia of Bible Difficulties* and Norman Geisler's and Thomas Howe's *When Critics Ask.* Though they are necessarily selective and not exhaustive, these books do show many creative approaches to difficult apparent discrepancies.

20. Another Ten Commandments?

"Is it a coincidence that the set of commandments in Exodus 34 happens to number ten, like the better known Ten Commandments of Exodus 20?"

Like you, every time I read Exodus 34 I too wonder what the significance of these "ten commandments" is. At the Biblical Archaeology Seminar (in Boston, November 19–21, 2000), I attended a lecture on the Ten Commandments, or Decalogue ("ten words")—including Exodus 20, Deuteronomy 5 and Exodus 34—by Michael Coogan. (He was in fact one of my Hebrew teachers at Harvard twenty years earlier.) He maintained that the Ten Commandments originally circulated in different forms. Scholars sometimes call the Exodus 34 list the "Ritual Decalogue," as opposed to the "Ethical Decalogue" of chapter 20. In other words, your observation has not gone unnoticed by scholars. But why is this Decalogue so similar and yet so different from the original?

A good rule of thumb whenever we are stuck in our understanding of a Bible passage is this: Examine the context. After the earlier giving of the law in chapter 20, along with its amplification in the chapters that follow, Israel had fallen into gross idolatry (chapter 32). Moses had shattered the first covenant. Chapter 34 is a sort of renewal of the covenant, a strong warning against returning to the temptations of Canaanite idolatry. This section of Exodus deliberately imitates the original Decalogue—ten words of warning to urge moral, doctrinal and religious purity in undivided devotion to Yahweh. From chapter 35 to the end of Exodus we read of the obedience of Moses and the Israelites in constructing the tabernacle, faithfully and "according to the book."

Thus, this second edition of the covenant serves a triple function: a *rebuke* after the idolatrous incident of chapter 32 (the golden calf/bull), a *recap* of God's distinctive covenant requirements and a *reminder* to holy living, which anticipates Leviticus in its gravity and specificity.

Incidentally, many scholars recognize the reason that there were *two* tablets was not that they would not all fit onto one tablet, but that covenants were normally written out in duplicate—one copy for each party. In this case, one copy was Israel's, one was God's.

21. Moral Teachings in John

"In my university Bible class, my professor stated that there were no moral teachings in the book of John—also that the book of John is merely an interpretation of the gospel, proclaiming Jesus' divinity. Would that mean that if you want to really hold to his teachings, you have to get those teachings from the first three Gospels?"

To begin with, this statement simply is not true. Though there are no "sin lists" in John, such as those we find in Matthew 15 and Mark 7, there are numerous challenges to morality in this Gospel. So fear not, you will not be forced to retreat to the first three Gospels for moral teaching!

In fact, I too recently heard this allegation in a lecture. Afterward, I went respectfully to the professor with a few written questions—my objections. I mentioned that, for example, in John 5 the Lord tells the man he healed at the Pool of Bethesda to "stop sinning." I have yet to receive any response.

22. Sacrificing Women

"In Judges 19:22–28, I don't understand why they would offer the women instead of just ignoring those guys or leaving? Also, in Judges 21:10–11, did the women and children have to die? I have read other passages as well that say to put everyone to death, and it seems like only one person had committed the sin."

The Bible tells it "like it is"—or—"like it was." It's not always pretty! But recording an event in the Scriptures is not the same thing as approving of it. This is an important point to keep in mind. It would seem that in Judges 19 leaving was not an option. It also appears that these fellows valued the lives of women less than the lives of men—even though the Bible makes clear from the outset that this is not right (Genesis 1:26–27, Galatians 3:28–29). Finally, in ancient times, it was customary (despite Ezekiel 18) to put whole families to death when the principal guilty party was the father.

23. Balaam

"I have been studying the book of Jude and I came across a verse which compares the godless men of Jude 4 to Balaam (Jude 11). So, I figured I would find out more about Balaam and what he did that was so bad. After reading the account of Balaam in Numbers 22–24, I can't understand why Balaam is looked at in such a bad light. Joshua 24:9–10 gives the impression that Balaam went through with cursing the Israelites, but he never did. And in Numbers 22:20–22 God tells Balaam to go with the men to talk with Balak, but when he goes, God gets angry with him. Please help me to understand this situation. Is there something I am missing?"

I too have wondered why Balaam gets such a bad rap in the New Testament. Since I have already written about this in *Life to the Full,* I will keep my remarks short. (You can see what I thought in the chapters on 2 Peter and Jude, both of which mention Balaam.)

Apart from the indication in Numbers that Balaam was killed because of his role in leading the Israelites into compromise (idolatry and sexual sin—Numbers 25), I agree that it is hard to see the pernicious motives in the Balaam cycle of the Old Testament which are attributed to him in the general epistles of the New Testament. And yet this is what the word of God says. Balaam played with fire, and he got burned.

24. Mustard Seeds

"In Mark 4:31 and Matthew 13:32, Jesus refers to the mustard seed as the smallest of seeds, yet in fact the orchid seed is the smallest seed. Could you please help me make sense of this so I can explain it to people who are eager to disprove the Bible and Jesus? Could it have just been the smallest in Palestine that grew to be the largest?"

The superlative is not necessarily meant to be taken literally. If Jesus cared nothing about being relatable to his Palestinian audience, he could have named the eucalyptus tree, whose miniscule seed produces a tree up to three hundred feet tall! But he didn't, presumably for the same reason the Bible never mentions koala bears and kangaroos—these were not familiar to his audience.

The Bible contains a good deal of hyperbole—and so does our everyday speech. When we are reading easy-going, colloquial language, we need to pay attention not only to the meanings of words, but also to the *feel* of the passage. In this case, the feel may be as follows: "The mustard seed—the smallest seed you've ever seen—illustrates what the kingdom of God is like...."

On the other hand, if people are *eager* to disprove the Bible and discredit Jesus, there may be little you can say that will convince them. They have to be willing, deep down in their innermost being, to follow truth wherever it may lead (John 7:17). Still, it is good and right to silence the criticisms with a to-the-point, respectful answer. I hope this helps!

25. Fourteen Generations?

"Matthew 1:17 says there were fourteen generations from Jeconiah to Jesus, but by my count there are only twelve. Matthew does have fourteen generations from Abraham to David and another fourteen from David to the Exile, but did he do his math wrong from the Exile to Jesus?"

Quite a few people have pointed this out, and some anti-Christian speakers have harped on the apparent discrepancy in an effort to weaken the faith of believers. You will notice the character at the start of the third section, Jeconiah. Who is he? He is King Jehoiakim. If you are familiar with the accounts in Kings and Chronicles, you are already wondering, has someone skipped Jehoiachin, the next to rule? The answer is quite simple.

The Hebrew scriptures often refer to Jehoiakim and Jehoiachin by the same name, "Jeconiah." The Greek translation of the Hebrew scriptures, the common Bible of the early Christians, used both "Jeconiah" and "Jehoiakim" for both Jehoiakim and Jehoiachin. Matthew, whose Gospel has come to us in Greek, uses "Jeconiah," which in essence is *two* kings, not one. Thus there are fourteen generations, inclusive, from Jeconiah to Christ, just as the Bible says.

26. Apocryphal References

"Who is being referred to in Hebrews 11:35, 37? Where can we read about someone being sawn in two? Who refused to be released to obtain a better resurrection? I can't seem to find the references anywhere in my Bible."

The reason you cannot find the passages is that the references are to extra-Biblical literature. (*Extra* means "outside," so "extra-Biblical" means "outside the Bible.") The better resurrection seems to be referring to the second century BC account in 2 Maccabees 7, the martyrdom of the mother and her seven sons. The books of the Maccabees have in fact been included in Catholic Bibles since around 400 AD, though Protestants reject them. I think it goes without saying that a book need not be completely true to be of some value. In fact there is much in the Apocrypha that is of great historical value, even though many parts of the apocryphal writings fall short in the areas of accuracy and inspiration. For more on the Apocrypha, see my essay in *Q & A*.

As for the question about the poor fellow who was sawn in two, I think the source is the Martyrdom of Isaiah. Here I find, "Because of these visions, therefore, Beliar was angry with Isaiah, and he dwelt in the heart of Manasseh, and he sawed Isaiah in half with a wood saw" (Martyrdom of Isaiah 5:1). Of course it is possible that someone else was sawn in two, but based on the limited information we have, Isaiah seems to be our best bet. For a complete collection of the pseudepigraphal (false authorship) works, see the two-volume set, *The Old Testament Pseudepigrapha*.[4]

27. Jude and Enoch

"How come the book of Enoch is quoted in Jude 14, but is not part of the Bible?"

The book of Enoch is quoted verbatim in Jude. What does this mean? Here are the possibilities:

- Jude believed the portion of Enoch he was quoting was correct, but not necessarily the rest of the work.
- Jude believed the entire book of Enoch was inspired, but he was wrong.
- Jude thought the entire book of Enoch was inspired, and the inclusion of Jude in the New Testament suggests he was right.

Before deciding which possibility is likeliest, let's proceed logically. The New Testament is full of quotations from a number of ancient works, some written by believers, some by nonbelievers (see chart). For example, Paul's speech on Mars Hill (the Areopagus) has at least five allusions to or citations of pagan writers. Would anyone consider Paul to believe that these writers were inspired? Unlikely. But the case of Jude is a little different, since Enoch is not an unbeliever, but the Old Testament man of faith who is described briefly in Genesis 5 and also in Hebrews 11. Nevertheless, citation from an ancient work no more proves its inspiration than a preacher's quotation of a modern poem or song suggests he takes the whole work as infallible.

The book of Enoch has survived in the ancient Ethiopic language (forty manuscripts) and fragmentarily in Aramaic, Greek and Latin, so we don't have to guess what the writer of 1 Enoch believed. His doctrine shines through in the writing. There is much to commend in the book of Enoch, and it reflects a thought world not unfamiliar to the New Testament writers. Yet, as I study it, I am not persuaded of its inspiration. For these reasons, I reject the possibility of its inspiration. Enoch's being cited is no compelling reason for the entire work being included in the Bible. The possibility of the first option bulleted above seems probable, although the theological implications of the second view are not particularly serious. You must weigh the evidence and make your own decision.

See the charts on the following pages.

Extra-Biblical References
Old Testament

Source Cited	Bible Passage
The Book of the Wars of the Lord	Numbers 21:14
The Poets	Numbers 21:27
The Book of the Annals of the Kings of Media and Persia	Esther 10:2
The Book of Jashar	Joshua 10:13, 2 Samuel 1:18
The Sayings of the Wise	Proverbs 22:17–24:34
The Sayings of Agur	Proverbs 30:1–33
The Sayings of King Lemuel	Proverbs 31:1
The Book of the Annals of the Kings of Israel	1 Kings 14:19, 15:31, 16:5, 16:14, 16:20, 16:27, 22:39; 2 Kings 1:18, 10:34, 13:8, 13:12, 14:15, 14:28, 15:11, 15:15, 15:21, 15:26, 15:31; 2 Chronicles 33:18
The Book of the Annals of the Kings of Judah	1 Kings 14:29, 15:7, 15:23, 22:45; 2 Kings 8:23, 12:19, 14:18, 15:6, 15:36, 16:19, 20:20, 21:17, 21:25, 23:28, 24:5
The Book of the Kings of Judah and Israel	2 Chronicles 16:11, 25:26, 28:26, 32:32
The Annotations of the Prophet Iddo	2 Chronicles 13:22
The Vision of the Prophet Isaiah	2 Chronicles 32:32
Genealogical Records	Nehemiah 7:5b, Ezra 2
The Book of the Annals of Solomon	1 Kings 11:41
The Book of the Annals of King David	1 Chronicles 27:24
The Records of Samuel the Seer	1 Chronicles 29:29
The Records of Nathan the Prophet	1 Chronicles 29:29
The Records of Gad the Seer	1 Chronicles 29:29
The Visions of Iddo the Seer	2 Chronicles 9:29
The Prophecy of Ahijah the Shilonite	2 Chronicles 9:29
The Annals of Jehu son of Hanani	2 Chronicles 20:34
The Letter of Elijah to Jehoram	2 Chronicles 21:12–15
The Annotations on the Book of the Kings	2 Chronicles 24:27
The Laments of Jeremiah for Josiah	2 Chronicles 35:25

Notes

- It is always possible that some of these sources may be identical to other sources, although with a different name.
- This is probably not a complete list.
- This study makes it clear that the Bible frequently quotes sources, without necessarily making those sources "inspired."

Extra-Biblical References
New Testament

Source Cited	Bible Passage
Epimenides of Knossos (De Oraculis/Peri Chresmon)	Titus 1:12
Epimenides of Soli	Acts 17:28a
Aratus the Cilician (Phaenomena 5, cp. Cleanthes frag. 537)	Acts 17:28b
Heraclitus	2 Peter 2:22b
The Assumption of Moses	Jude 9
The Book of Enoch	Jude 14–15

Possible Allusions:

Euripides (fragment 968)	Acts 17:24
Euripides (Heracles 1345–36)	Acts 17:25
Euripides (Bacchae 794)	Acts 26:14
Julianus (Or. 8, 246b)	Acts 26:14
Menander (Thais)	1 Corinthians 15:33 (see also Isaiah 22:13)
Thucydides (II 97, 4)	Acts 20:35

Notes

- Unknown—1 Corinthians 4:6, Ephesians 5:14. Most scholars believe Ephesians 5:14 is a fragment of an ancient Christian baptismal hymn.
- There are many more possible parallels to NT verses in Greco-Roman literature.
- In addition, there are scores of allusions to the Old Testament Apocrypha in the New Testament, although no direct quotations.

28. Lying Okay?

"I have a question that has been bothering my heart. I have been studying the book of Joshua. In the second chapter Rahab lies, and this seems to be okay because of the situation. I am quite confused. Can you help me to find information about the book of Joshua and help me to understand the situation?"

Rahab is commended in Hebrews 11 for her faith. She sided with the people of God and did her best to support the Israelites (Joshua 2:1–7). Yet, she is not commended for lying per se. The book of Joshua reports what happened as it happened. It does not always offer a value judgment on what is happening.

Sometimes we say things or do things which may not fully conform to the moral will of God, yet we are blessed anyway because of our heart. Once again, Rahab is nowhere praised for her lying. Yet by her faith she saved not only herself, but her family as well. She ranks with the great women of faith, despite her moral failings, her previous lifestyle and even those imperfections arising in the course of her striving to do right.

29. 'Coming Soon' in Revelation

"At least four times in Revelation, Jesus says 'I am coming soon.' In the Bible, 'soon' usually doesn't mean two-thousand-plus years later. Is there a scripture in the Bible that actually directly ties the Second Coming or return of Jesus with the end of the world? Is Revelation describing some figurative way in which the Lord has already returned?"

I would take a look at passages like Hebrews 9:27 and 2 Thessalonians 1:8–10. These are just two of the passages that tie the return of Christ with judgment. I understand Revelation to provide a picture of the judgment of God's enemies, the vindication of his saints, the punishment of the wicked and the eternal reward of the righteous. Yet Revelation also has a historical context, and the "coming" of Jesus in this book can also be understood as God's coming in judgment against the Roman Empire, through a series of plagues, wars and invasions, as well as through "foes within."

In Daniel 8:26, the "distant future" is a span of less than four centuries (around 530 BC to 165 BC). You are right; why should "soon" in Revelation 1:1–3 mean six or more times as long? To sum up, I believe that Revelation sheds light on the ultimate fate of the wicked and the reward of the saints. Yet it has a specific historical fulfillment. All disciples should live in a state of preparedness for the coming of the Lord, which may take place at any time. Yet in one sense, for the persecuting Roman Empire, "judgment day" came many centuries ago. For more on the book of Revelation, see Gordon Ferguson's *Mine Eyes Have Seen the Glory*.[5]

30. The Sin of the Census

"Why was David's taking a census of Israel a sin in 2 Samuel 24 and 1 Chronicles 21? I looked up 'census' in my concordance and found Exodus 30:11–13: 'When you take a census of the Israelites to count them, each one must pay the Lord a ransom for his life at the time he is counted. Then no plague will come on them when you number them.' But I'm still not sure why taking the census was a sin. Any ideas?"

You were wise to consult your concordance, since the punishment David chose for his sin was the very punishment Exodus specified. This implies that Joab and the census committee failed to take up the census tax. Yet the real point of the passages in Samuel and Chronicles is theological. It is wrong to rely on the flesh rather than on God, to put confidence in numbers rather than in the Spirit.

There are applications for us today. When we strive for growth at all costs, we risk being opposed by God himself, just as David was some three thousand years ago. We need to learn to trust God, without trying to guarantee success through numerical games and reliance on analysis and statistics. God will bless his kingdom, steer it and prosper it—even when circumstances are contrary or we lack a sense of direction or times are tough.

31. Only 144,000 in Heaven?

"Is it true that the Bible says only 144,000 people will be allowed into heaven?"

This misunderstanding is based on an overliteral reading of the book of Revelation, which is a prophetic work full of symbolism. Chapters 7 and 14 of Revelation use the symbolic number 144,000 to refer to God's redeeming of his people. If we took the number literally, which in a book like Revelation would be highly unwise, then we would be obligated to take every element of the passage literally. Look closely at Revelation 7:4 and 14:4. We see that the redeemed are (1) Jews only, though not from the tribe of Dan, (2) males only and (3) virgins only. In other words, unless you are a celibate, Jewish male not descended from Dan, you have no hope of heaven. I am quite sure that my female readers would disapprove of such an interpretation, but probably more than ninety-nine percent of my male readers would also reject the literalistic understanding.

The 144,000 simply refers symbolically to the full number of the redeemed who will be in heaven.[6]

Notes

[1] This table is adapted from a lecture at the 2000 Biblical Archaeology Seminar in Nashville by Eric H. Cline. It can also be found in Cline's *The Battles of Armageddon: Megiddo and the Jezreel Valley from the Bronze Age to the Nuclear Age* (University of Michigan Press, 2000).

[2] Lutheran theologian and pastor, 1582–1651. His German name was Peter Meiderlin. "Rupertus" and "Meldenius" constitute his publication name—anagrams of his names in Latin!

[3] Editor's note: "To knock for a six" is an English idiom that has its origins in the game of cricket. It means "to baffle, confound."

[4] James H. Charlesworth, ed., *The Old Testament Pseudepigrapha* (Garden City, N.Y.: Doubleday, 1983).

[5] Gordon Ferguson, *Mine Eyes Have Seen the Glory* (Billerica, Mass.: Discipleship Publications International, 1996).

[6] For more on the symbolism of numbers in the book of Revelation, see Gordon Ferguson, *Mine Eyes Have Seen the Glory* (Billerica, Mass.: Discipleship Publications International, 1996).

3
Basic Bible

1. Meaning of 'Bible'

"What does the word 'Bible' mean? Ironically, I can't find the word anywhere in my Bible."

Good observation. The word "Bible" does not appear in the Bible. (Some religious groups have a slogan, "Bible names for Bible things." By this criterion, however, even the word "Bible" would be excluded!) The word comes from the Greek *biblion/biblia*. In Greek, *ta biblia* simply means "the books," as in English *bibliography*. The Bible, as we know, is a library of sixty-six life-giving volumes.

2. Bible Dictionaries and Concordances

"Which Bible dictionary and concordances do you prefer or recommend? There are so many out there, and I'd like to buy a few solid Bible tools."

Let me refer you to the Bible Reference Tools section of the Acesonline.org Web site. Also useful would be Steve Kinnard's book, *Getting the Most from the Bible*, which references a number of useful works.[1]

3. The Book of Esther

"Is it true that the book of Esther is suspect because it does not mention God?"

Although the word "God" does not appear in the book of Esther, God himself is implicit in the fabric of the narrative. God is protecting his people through the courage of Esther and Mordecai; God causes the sleepless king to call for the archived record of Mordecai's service to the Persian Empire; and God is the one who brings about justice for Haman and the Jewish people alike. Yes, for some the absence of the word "God" makes the entire book of Esther suspect. For believers, though, who through the eyes of faith are able to recognize what is really going on behind the scenes, the book is brimming over with God and his Spirit.

4. Big Bang

"Isn't the big bang theory against the Bible?"

Actually, there is much in the big bang theory that agrees with the Bible! This theory, formulated in the first half of the twentieth century, suggests that space and time had an actual beginning. Though the theory is complex, its simplicity is astounding: everything we see all began in a single moment in the distant past. In the big bang theory, as has often been noted, science and theology converge. Before the theory was proposed—empirical confirmation came only in 1965—most scientists supposed the universe was infinitely old. Yet the big bang shows us that the universe has a beginning. And what is "before" this beginning? God is! (And I say that if he chose to bring the cosmos into existence through a well-designed explosion, that is his business.)

5. Meaning of 'Jesus Christ'

"What does 'Jesus Christ' actually mean?"

"Jesus" means "salvation." In both Hebrew *(Yehoshua)* and Greek *(Yesous)*, this is the same word as "Joshua." "Christ" is from the Greek *Christos,* "anointed one," which corresponds to the Hebrew for Messiah *(Masshiah).* Of course "Christ" is a title, not a last name!

6. Jesus and the Logos

"If Jesus is the Logos, then the Word of God came to earth in the flesh. The Bible is the inspired word of God and speaks his will to us when we read it. How then are they related? The Bible didn't die for my sins. Jesus isn't written

> down on paper for reference. The two are different entities,
> but both are called the 'Word' of God. I keep finding
> myself equating the two, and I am not sure if this is right."

Yes, the Word (logos) and the Word (Bible) are related,
but they are not exactly the same, as you have figured
out.[2] There are too many contradictions for this to be true.
So, think about them as connected, but separate. One
connecting passage that people often miss is Proverbs 8,
which talks about God's wisdom. Then 1 Corinthians 1:24
says that Christ is our wisdom. He was also an agent in creation at the very beginning, as the language of Proverbs 8,
John 1 and Colossians 1 also attest. Certainly, the words of
the Bible are an inspired revelation from God. For this reason we can accurately call the Bible the word of God.
Jesus, too, is a revelation of God—all the fullness of the
deity in human form (Colossians 2:9).

The idea of the "Word of God" is rich in significance.
We are told that God brought all of Creation into existence
by his word: "Let there be… and there was…" (Genesis 1).
When the Bible speaks of Jesus as the Word of God, it is
hinting at the close association between a speaker and his
words. In one sense, you *are* what you say; what you say
is the *expression* of who you are. In another sense, you *are
not* precisely the same thing as your words. This subtle
"connected but separate," "same but different" quality that
is associated with the idea of "the Word" makes it a fitting
analogy for the relationship between the Father and the
Son—both God, and yet somehow different from each
other—that forms the essence of the doctrine of the trinity.

7. Was Joseph Really Jesus' Father?

"Was Joseph really Jesus' father? Matthew 1:16 says he was
the husband of Mary, who was the mother of Jesus. How
should we understand this passage?"

Your question is a good one. Joseph is not Jesus' father—at least biologically. Yet legally, he was indeed Jesus' father, and in the ancient mentality, legal paternity was sufficient to confer hereditary rights. As Christians, we believe that Mary came to be with child through the Holy Spirit. She was fully Jesus' biological mother. And yet Jesus Christ, the "God-man," was also truly the Son of God.

8. What Happened to Joseph?

"Is there any Biblical indication of what happened to Joseph, Mary's husband? Is there any early church tradition that seems valid?"

I assume you are referring to the conspicuous absence of Joseph at the time of Jesus' public ministry. The most common understanding, I believe, is that Joseph died before Jesus began his ministry. This makes sense, especially since Jesus entrusts his mother to the apostle John at the time of his crucifixion (John 19:26–27). Why would he have done this if his father were still alive? (Presumably his four younger brothers were married and all had their own families; John was therefore more available.)

9. The Gospel of Thomas

"I understand that the apostle Thomas traveled as far as India, but I am not so sure whether or not he was the one who wrote the Gospel of Thomas. Should this book be in the Bible?"

Indeed, tradition is strong that the apostle Thomas established the church in India sometime in the 40s AD. Although I began by being skeptical about this involvement, I have read enough now to be fairly convinced. I have even seen Thomas' tomb in south India. There seems little reason to doubt the veracity of the tradition. However, the "gospel" attributed to him is another matter.

The Gospel of Thomas is increasingly popular these days, especially among people who want us to believe that the New Testament is not a complete or accurate record of what Jesus taught during his earthly ministry. Actually, this book, or collection of supposed sayings of Jesus, is not really a "gospel" at all, since the Passion narrative is totally absent. There is no emphasis either on self-sacrificing love, except possibly one saying about carrying one's cross. Unlike the four canonical Gospels, the book by Thomas is only a list of sayings.

Before I present an assortment of passages from the Gospel of Thomas, let me reiterate that I doubt strongly that Thomas is in any way responsible for its creation. The theology of the book, if there is a real theology, is Gnostic. For example, insight is more important than morality, spirit more real and significant than matter. Gnosticism is making a comeback today in the New Age Movement. This was a philosophy-religion that appealed to the ego, without requiring any real commitment.

Manuscripts of this book, complete or partial, have been found from the second and third centuries, so the Gospel of Thomas was probably written no later than about 100 or 150 AD, and may possibly date to the first century. The Bible reader will recall that as early as Paul's own lifetime, Gnosticism was a growing threat to the nascent church. (See, for example, 1 Timothy, which is full of warnings about the Gnostic teachers. Note that *gnosis* is the Greek word for "knowledge," as in 1 Timothy 6:20.)

The numbering of the following excerpts may vary slightly from edition to edition, but given the shortness of the Gospel of Thomas, you should have no trouble locating the original sayings if you decide to go further in your study. (See chart on the following pages.)

So, is the New Testament missing any books? Not at all. Nothing is "missing," because nothing was removed or lost. Quite simply, the early church did not recognize the authority of this "gospel"—nor has any part of Christianity subsequently.

Excerpts from the Gospel of Thomas

Prologue

"These are the secret sayings that the living Jesus spoke and Judas Thomas the Twin recorded." Here is purported to be a "secret" source for a competing tradition about Jesus. Fragments of the Gospel of Thomas were discovered in the late 1800s, and by 1945 the Egyptian desert had begun to yield more or less complete copies. By reading these sayings, the writer claims that you enter an elite circle who know what Jesus really said.

Arcane Sayings

A number of sayings in the Gospel of Thomas seem to defy analysis. What did they mean? What was their original context? While explanations have been offered, no one really knows what the writer—whoever he was—meant to convey. For example, consider the following two sayings.

- *Saying 3: "Jesus said, 'The kingdom is inside you and outside you.'"*
- *Saying 7: "Jesus said, 'Happy is the lion whom the man eats, so that the lion becomes a man; but woe to the man whom the lion eats, so that the man becomes lion!'"*

In short, because we do not understand what these sayings refer to, *and* because they are lacking the literary and historical contexts that would give us the necessary clues, they must remain shrouded in mystery. For all intents and purposes, they are arcane.

Authentic Sayings?

Some of the sayings found in the Gospel of Thomas may be the actual words of Jesus, or reflect genuine teachings of the apostles. While of course it is not possible to prove any particular saying is authentic, with a little imagination it is easy to envision quite a few of them as Jesus' original words.

- *Saying 2: "Jesus said, 'Let not him who seeks desist until he finds. When he finds he will be troubled; when he is troubled he will marvel, and he will reign over the universe.'"*

- *Saying 47: "A person cannot mount two horses or bend two bows, and a servant cannot serve two lords."*
- *Saying 64: "Business people and merchants will not enter the realm of my Father." (This saying appears at the end of this version of the Parable of the Banquet. The beginning of the story is not especially problematic, despite its rather disturbing ending.)*
- *Saying 98: "Give Caesar what is Caesar's, give God what is God's, and give me what is mine!"*

Once again, since not all of Jesus' words were recorded in the Scriptures (John 21:25), there is no reason to think that some of them could not have found their way into various sayings sources. Yet who will assess whether they are authentic?

Absurd Sayings

The following three sayings reflect the Gnosticism of the early heretics, and the middle one appears to be pantheistic. ("Pantheism" is the doctrine that God *is* everything.) It is highly unlikely that Jesus is the one behind any of them.

- *Saying 67: "Jesus said, 'He who knows the All and has no need but of himself has need everywhere.'"*
- *Saying 77: "Jesus said, 'I am the light which shines upon all. I am the All; All has gone forth from me and All has come back to me. Cleave the wood, and there am I; raise the stone, and there you will find me.'"*
- *Saying 113–114: "Simon Peter said to them, 'Let Mary leave us, because women are not worthy of life.' Jesus said, 'Behold, I shall guide her so as to make her male, so that she may become a living spirit like you men. For every woman who makes herself male will enter the kingdom of heaven.'"*

Next time your friends or workmates drop comments about the Gospel of Thomas, hopefully you will now be well equipped to respond. If you are interested in further reading, translations from the original Coptic are easily obtainable.[3]

10. Luke 6:38 in the Chinese Bible

"I read the Chinese Bible. In a morning quiet time I came to Luke 6:38, where the word 'funnel' is used, whereas 'good measure' is used in the English Bible. They are really different, and I am wondering how to explain the difference."

Well, I am flattered, but I do not know a word of Chinese. Unless you are talking about menu Chinese—there I might be able to help you! But I have contacted my Chinese sources and am informed that:

> "Funnel" was the common instrument for measure in ancient China, and therefore this word is usually interchangeable with the word "measure." We can still use this word to describe measure today, even though we don't use the funnel to measure anymore.

11. Authorship of 1 and 2 Timothy

"I would like your personal opinion as a Bible scholar about the authorship of 1 and 2 Timothy. I read that many scholars believe these books were written after Paul's time by someone assuming Paul's name. What is your opinion?"

First, thanks for the compliment, but despite my study of theology, I am not a Biblical scholar. I rely on the work of the professionals who devote their full time to careful study of the Biblical documents.

In the 1800s, it was common for liberal scholars to claim that 1-2 Timothy and Titus (called the Pastoral Epistles, as they provide pastoral direction to a church leader) were penned in the mid-second century! They were said to reflect a later "stage" of development of the Christian community, the "early Catholic" church. It was denied that they could have been written by Paul because they discuss church organization and polity, which allegedly would not have been of interest in the first century, when everyone was expecting the imminent end of the world. In addition, as there are quite a few words in these letters which do not appear in Paul's other letters, his authorship was denied. Rather, someone was trying to tap into his authority by writing a pseudonymous epistle. Further, it is said the "style" of the letter is not that of the historical Paul.

My response is to vigorously deny all these claims. First, even though many first century believers may have expected the day of judgment in their lifetime, that did not stop them from appointing leaders and providing for the next generation. See, for example, Paul's speech concerning the future of the flock, made to the Ephesian elders in Acts 20; the existence in Philippians 1:1 of elders and servants/ministers (presbyters and deacons, by transliteration from the Greek); and the concern for *future* generations in Ephesians 3:20–21. Numerous NT passages make clear that Paul was intentionally laying a foundation for subsequent generations—so that each one would be ready for the Lord's return, whenever that was to take place.

Would we not expect a different style—and even vocabulary—in a document written from one church leader to another? It is not, after all, written to the members in general. It is more like an "internal memo," meant to be understood by a recipient in a similar professional situation to the sender.

Finally, it was common to employ a professional scribe (or "amanuensis") when writing a letter. (See, for example, the reference to Tertius in 1 Corinthians 16:22.) We ought not to read too much into stylistic differences. Are we not allowed to change our own style? Must we always adhere to a single style? We possess so few of Paul's letters—only thirteen—that it is difficult to be dogmatic about how he must have written during the twenty or so year span during which he sent out his epistles.

Conservative scholars usually contend that 1 Timothy was written by Paul in the mid-60s AD, when the evangelist Timothy was leading the church at Ephesus. Titus is normally considered to have been written next, when this evangelist led the church on the island of Crete. Paul produced

2 Timothy shortly before his execution, probably around 68 AD. The Pastoral Epistles, in other words, are written by whom they claim to be written: Paul, the "apostle to the Gentiles," in his final years of fruitful service on earth.

12. The Elder

"When the Bible describes the qualifications of an elder, we are told he needs to be the, 'husband of one wife.' Does that mean he can only be married to one woman at a time, or that, regardless of reasons or circumstances, he can only have taken one wife during the course of his life?"

There are three ways to take the phrase you are referring to, which appears in 1 Timothy 3:2 and Titus 1:6.

- Monogamy, as opposed to polygamy. The passage is against multiple simultaneous marriages, which would disqualify a prospective elder.
- One wife, as opposed to a man who is remarried. The passage is against multiple consecutive marriages, which disqualify one from eldership.
- A virtuous life, manifested in fidelity to his wife. The passage approves of men who have been faithful to their wives.

Until recently I held that the passage concerned monogamy. Certainly in situations where there are multiple wives the dysfunction of the family rules out eldership! Sometimes it is claimed the Old Testament encourages polygamy. I would say just the opposite. Not only is the "one man, one wife" model presented as normative in Genesis 1–2, but polygamous situations in Genesis are portrayed as awkward, unharmonious and friction-filled. This view might be right, except for the following consideration.

The identical Greek construction ("one-woman man") appears in 1 Timothy 3:2 and in 1 Timothy 5:9 (though inverted), in reference to the older woman who might qualify for assistance on the widows' list ("one-man woman"). If a woman had remarried after her husband died, she would be disqualified were her second husband to die! Doesn't sound fair, does it? Nor does the second option. How would the death of a spouse, for example, which led to your entering a second marriage, disqualify you for eldership?

The third option seems likeliest. The "one-woman man" is the married man who has not bought into the world's values—he has not cheated. Only such a man may contemplate the high calling of the eldership.

13. Jesus' Birth

"When was Jesus born? I have heard that it was in the summer, then recently I heard it was in October. How do you know the answer?"

Even the early Christians admitted that they had no idea which month Jesus was born in! Yet the Bible does give a few clues. Shepherds were out in the fields with their sheep. This would not have been normal behavior in the rainy season (around November to March). Besides, the government was conducting a census, which involved many families traveling to their ancestral villages. This would have been difficult in the cold, rainy season. So, this seems to rule out December. Actually, December 25 was the "birthday" of the Persian god Mithras, which by transference became Jesus' "birthday"—though not till the third century. So, it doesn't look too good for the traditional date. To answer your question: you can't know the answer. Therefore, you are free to celebrate it whenever you like—why not every day?

14. Egypt and Rome

"I just finished reading Revelation. As the seven plagues were being unleashed on the earth, the inhabitants, although in pain and some awfully hurt, kept on cursing God and 'shaking their fists' at him. I remember also reading that during the plagues on Egypt prior to the Israelites' being released, Pharaoh's heart was hardened. Am I wrong in drawing what seems to be an obvious parallel here? I understood that with Pharaoh, the Bible states that God hardened his heart. In Revelation, on the other hand, no such intervention by God occurred."

Good observation. Yes indeed, there are parallels:

- Neither Pharaoh with his magicians nor the enemies of God in Revelation repented, despite ample incentives.
- In neither situation does God contravene human free will. This he is consistently unwilling to do.

However, I am not so sure God did not harden his enemies' hearts in Revelation. In fact, I believe that whenever we decide to harden our hearts, God goes ahead and does the hardening. (When we place soft clay in an oven, the oven hardens the clay—and yet at the same time it is also true that we are hardening the clay.) In theological terms, the hardening on God's part and that on our part are concurrent. In other words, God may not have intervened in Pharaoh's case at all—at least not beyond the parameters of his normal mode of operation.

15. Soul and Spirit

"In Hebrews 4:12–13 what is the difference between soul and spirit? Is this human spirit or Holy Spirit?"

In Hebrews 4, "spirit" refers to the human spirit. The sword penetrates the heart, dividing (human) soul from (human) spirit. Is this a poetic way of describing the state of unpreparedness on Judgment Day, or is something deeper indicated? It is hard to say.

In the Bible, "soul" refers to the entire person (body and spirit), whereas "spirit" is the spiritual part of the individual. Many volumes have been written about Biblical psychology and pneumatology (the theological areas which are involved in the "long" answer to your question). I hope you are satisfied with my short answer!

16. Tithing

"Is it true that the word 'tithe' doesn't appear once in the New Testament? I looked but I may have missed it. If it doesn't, does that mean that God no longer requires it and rather encourages it only as a way to help out the less fortunate of the world?"

The word "tithe" is related to the word "tenth," and they mean the same. You will find the word *tenth* in most modern English Bibles (as in Matthew 23:23 and Hebrews 7:1–10). And yet each occurrence refers to the practice of tithing *under the old covenant*. This is an important distinction. Nowhere does the NT command us to give ten percent—not that I am opposed (in general) to the practice. For more on this matter, see my first volume of *Q & A,* page 100.

17. Footnotes

"I have a question about the footnotes in the Bible. Often we read something like 'the meaning of the Hebrew for this word is uncertain.' What does that mean? If the translators don't know what the Hebrew word meant for sure, how can we clearly understand the passage in English? (One specific example is Job 21:24.)"

First, let us commend translators whenever they honestly admit uncertainty. Translation from one language into another is rarely an absolutely certain enterprise, since there may be a range of meanings for a given word in the original language, as well as several ways to accurately express an idea in the translation language. Yet ninety-nine percent of all sentences in the Old Testament are fairly certain, as a comparison of alternate translations quickly makes clear. It is better to "be real" than to confidently pretend knowledge. Yet once again, there are relatively few words in the 31,000 verses of the Bible whose meanings elude us.

Since you mention Job 21, let us use this as a window into the sometimes challenging world of Bible translation. The sense of Job 21:24 is clear enough: the person is well-nourished, even though he may not be a God-fearing individual. (Healthiness of marrow is also mentioned in Proverbs 3:8.) The Hebrew word in question seems to appear only once in the Old Testament, adding to the confusion. Here is how some of the translations read:

> ...his sides are filled out with fat, and the marrow of his bones is moist. (NAS)
> ...his breasts (or milk pails) are full of milk, and his bones are moistened with marrow. (KJV)
> ...his body well nourished, his bones rich with marrow. (NIV)
> ...his body full of fat and the marrow of his bones moist. (RSV)
> ...viscera eius plena sunt adipe et medullis ossa illius inrigantur. (Latin: His entrails are full of fat and the bones of this one are moistened with marrow.)

All translations yield the same general sense; the confusion centers only around one word, the Hebrew *'atin,* meaning "milk pail" or "bucket." We are dealing with figurative language (nearly the entire book of Job is poetry, as the NIV indentations and stanzas indicate). One can see that the NIV follows the RSV, avoiding too specific a translation of *'atin.* The NAS similarly uses a broad word, "sides." The Latin *viscera* conveys the same sense as the NAS, while the KJV humorously over-interprets, leading to a biological implausibility.

But whichever the correct translation, no doctrine of scripture depends on it, nor is the gist of the passage substantially affected. This is typical of verses for which the translators have expressed doubt as to the perfect rendering of obscure Hebrew words. And while I personally read every footnote, there is nothing wrong with a Bible reader skipping them entirely. Little will be missed.

18. Italicization

"A friend of the family asked me a Bible question I couldn't answer: Why do so many translations have random words italicized? This is distracting and makes the Bible so hard to read. I told him that I didn't know, but that I would investigate. My instinct was that it has to do with the language of the time when the translation was done, so I checked every Bible in my house. I opened a KJV Bible to Isaiah 64 and found sixteen fairly randomly italicized words. I checked a Jerusalem Bible—no italics. NIV—no italics. Spanish Bible—no italics. French Bible—no italics. Why would this be?"

First, these words are not *randomly* italicized. The translators (of the King James Version, for example) are indicating that for the sake of clarity they are supplying words *not in the original*. The forewords, or prefaces, of most Bibles set out the principles upon which their translations have been made, as well as their conventions (paragraphing, italicization, spelling and so forth). It pays to read the preface before diving in to any version.

More literal versions italicize words for added clarity, and I think this is helpful for the reader—for the most part, anyway! In 1 Corinthians 12–14, the well-meaning KJV translators chose to render the Greek *glossai* (languages, or "tongues" in the English of around 1600) by two words: "*unknown* tongues." As you can see, the word *unknown* has been added; it is not present in the original Greek of 1 Corinthians. The problem is that many later readers, such as those who are part of the "charismatic movement" that began in the twentieth century, took this to mean that these languages were unknown on earth! You can see where this led. For more, see my book *The Spirit*.

19. NIV and KJV

"I studied the Bible with a friend of mine who reckons that the NIV does not contain the whole word of God because in some places it is different from the King James Bible. I want to know the reasons for those differences."

In America especially, there is hostility between the "NIV camp" and the "KJV camp." Tradition dies hard! Tell your friend the following facts:

- No translation is perfect. (Only the originals were perfect!)
- All versions differ from one another as a function both of legitimate translation decisions and of the generation in which the translation was made, because all languages are constantly changing.
- There were many good English translations before the KJV.
- The KJV has many errors because in the seventeenth century Biblical Hebrew and Koine Greek were not completely understood. Also, the major Greek papyrus discoveries were not made till the late nineteenth century, while the Hebrew Dead Sea Scrolls were not discovered until after World War II.
- Tell him that just as there are many people who stubbornly "defend" the King James, there are equally stubborn people who "defend" the NIV against all the newer translations (more recent than the 1970s when the NIV was completed).

If your friend reads books (hopefully his mind is open to reading books other than the Bible), recommend Neil Lightfoot's *From KJV to NIV*.[4] He will find it very helpful.

Most important, make sure your friend is diligently studying the Bible. Otherwise, a whole mountain of opinions is worthless. Beware of the Pharisaism that leads a person to say, "My version alone is right."

20. Date of the Exodus

"I've been doing research on the life of Joseph and am troubled by trying to pin down the approximate date of the Exodus. I'm thinking from all the study I've done that it's about 1440 BC. If this is so, it puts Joseph roughly in mid-eighteenth century BC. I'm not sure, however, if this coincides with the reign of the Hyksos rulers, and also which dynasty of Egyptian Pharaohs it would fall under. Bottom line, based on your study, when did the Exodus occur?"

Most scholars place the Exodus sometime in the 1400s or the 1200s BC, conservatives tending to favor the earlier time period. At face value, 1 Kings 6:1 seems to point to the fifteenth century date. Moreover, scholars are not all agreed that the "king who did not know Joseph" was Hyksos (Asiatic). I tend to favor the traditional date of 1446 BC, but I have sympathy for at least one of the alternative suggestions: 1290 BC. For more on this, see any OT survey, such as *Introducing the Old Testament*.[5]

21. Authorship of Hebrews

"Who do you think wrote the book of Hebrews, and why?"

No one really knows. Although the style is Pauline, suggesting that the letter was penned by someone in Paul's sphere of influence, I see no way to prove who wrote it, and no direct evidence that Paul wrote this fine epistle. Consider the following facts:

- The early church consistently admitted that "only God knows"[6] who wrote Hebrews. If they had no clue, why should we think our guesses are more likely to be on target?
- In the Middle Ages, the name of Paul somehow became attached to the beginning of the letter as a superscription.
- The author insists this is only a "*brief* word of exhortation" (13:22, emphasis mine). For Paul, this would have been one of his longer letters.
- Modern scholars have suggested many possible authors: Barnabas, Luke, Mary, Priscilla and many more. The most popular choice in our generation is actually Apollos—a man with the education level

evinced in Hebrews, as well as one who would have written in the Alexandrian style of this letter.

- This letter, unlike all other letters in the New Testament, gives no indication of who wrote it. Its anonymity is not a good platform upon which to construct a theory of authorship.

So, to answer your question, I do not know who wrote Hebrews. As to why, it is because the evidence is too slender to be confident of any one suggestion of authorship over another.

Notes

[1] Steve Kinnard, *Getting the Most from the Bible* (Billerica, Mass.: Discipleship Publications International, 2000).

[2] Editor's note: There is a method to our madness when it comes to capitalizing the word "word." When used to describe Jesus, "Word" is always capitalized. When designating the Bible, it is only capitalized if it is not modified. For example, "the Bible is the Word"; but "the Bible is the word of God."

[3] Try *The Secret Teachings of Jesus: Four Gnostic Gospels*, tr. Marvin W. Meyer (New York: Random House, 1984), or *Jesus and Christian Origins Outside the New Testament*, F. F. Bruce (London: Hodder & Stoughton, 1974).

[4] Jack Lewis, *The English Bible, from KJV to NIV: A History and Evaluation* (Grand Rapids: Baker, 1991).

[5] John Drane, *Introducing the Old Testament* (San Francisco: Harper & Row, 1987), 57–58.

[6] Origen, as quoted by Eusebius, *Historia Ecclesiae* VI.25.

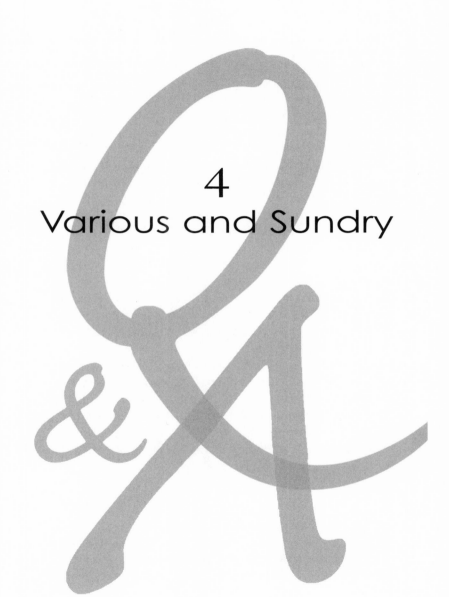

4
Various and Sundry

1. Women in Men's Clothing

"I don't understand Deuteronomy 22:5. A lot of women wear men's clothing!"

Some church groups teach that it is a sin for a woman to wear man's clothing and *vice versa*. The old law forbade this because it was the way of the pagans (the Canaanites), and God's people were to be separate and distinct. While I am not *personally* in favor of "cross-dressing"—primarily because it is usually associated with sexual perversion— there is no NT verse explicitly forbidding this sort of thing. OT commands do not apply to NT times unless they are repeated in the New Testament. Moreover, clothing styles change, and through the centuries they change drastically! (Have you ever looked at pictures of how men dressed just a few centuries ago? And have you ever seen how the ancient Roman men wore skirts?) In short, you understood Deuteronomy 22:5 quite well, only you struggled when you tried to apply this OT law to our situation today. But we live under a different law.

At the same time, I must add that God's word consistently upholds clear distinctions between the genders, from Genesis to Revelation. A denial of one's gender is offensive to God, who created us. Our society is manifesting increasing blurriness in its thinking about gender issues, to the great detriment of the family and insecurity of countless men and women alike.

2. Tattoos

"I would like to ask about tattoos. Leviticus 19:28 seems to argue against them. I realize this passage is in the context of OT law, to which we are not accountable. Are tattoos a matter of right and wrong? What does the Bible say about it?"

Tattoos, which were associated with idolatry, were apparently common among Canaanites and other peoples. It was for religious reasons, therefore, that the Jews were forbidden to put marks on their bodies. As tattoos these days (usually) have no religious significance, I can see no reason to disallow them, at least on Biblical grounds. You are right, the New Testament says nothing about them, and so we must consider this an area of freedom.

I would recommend that you not be too quick, though, to run out and get yourself tattooed. There may be a number of practical reasons for which this would not be wise.

3. Halloween

"We do not celebrate Halloween. It used to be my understanding that Satanists view Halloween as a special day. I have tried to research books, periodicals and the Internet on the subject of Halloween, however, and I have not been able to find evidence to support this allegation. In fact, I have not been able to find definitive, reliable information on the origins of Halloween at all. I do not want to have anything to do with Satanism, devil worship or witchcraft. What is your advice on this?"

I am glad you ask the question because a good number of churchgoers are of the opinion that Halloween is a serious compromise with the powers of darkness. My opinion is that Halloween is, for the most part, harmless fun. My advice is that each disciple should follow his own conscience and convictions based on Scripture.

Many features of modern life have roots in paganism: for example, the names of the days of the week and avoidance of the number thirteen. Does this mean I should refuse to use the "Thursday," lest I imply that the Nordic god Thor was real? Or that I should avoid hotels which—and I think this is juvenile!—skip the thirteenth floor? Is such a radical position realistic, necessary or even Biblical?

The origins of Halloween are not difficult to find; I would suggest another Internet search. You will see the connection with the ancient Irish pagan celebration of *Samhain*. Catholic tradition designates November 1 as "All

Saints Day" (in modern English) or "All Hallow Day" (in old English). Therefore they say that the devil chose the night before—"All Hallow Even" or "Hallowe'en"—as his special night of mischief. Today, Halloween is typically observed—apart from its crass American commercialism— by poking fun at the dark side. (At least with costumes of ghosts, witches and skeletons—not so much when kids dress up as Pinocchio, Aladdin or Anastasia!) In all my years I have never met anyone who went "trick or treating" in honor of Satan; they all did it for the sake of sweets! I suppose it would be possible to tour the neighborhoods with some sort of diabolical understanding, and that would clearly be wrong. But what's wrong with a costume party?

Your desire to avoid Satanism in any form is commendable. Galatians 5:21 tells us that witchcraft is sinful. And yet I do not see how a costume party—at the expense of Satan, in this case, who deserves to be mocked—is of any spiritual harm.

This is not to say that too light or flippant a treatment of the Evil One and his minions is not without its dangers. We should never underestimate the malevolence or malignancy of the Prince of Darkness.

4. Killing and Murder

"Exodus 20:13 and Deuteronomy 5:17 (NRSV) say 'You shall not murder,' with a footnote mentioning 'kill' as a substitute for 'murder.' In the New International Version they say, 'You shall not murder,' without any footnote giving 'kill' as an alternative for 'murder.' What does the original text say about 'murder' versus 'killing'? Biblically speaking, is it correct to define 'killing' as taking life, and 'murder' as illegal killing?"

The original text has the word *ratsach,* which means "to murder." *Harag* is one word meaning "kill," but it is not used in these particular verses.

5. Suicide

"Did Jesus commit suicide for us? (Why or why not?) Is it really considered suicide to 'take a bullet' for someone else?"

Allowing oneself to be killed is not the same as taking one's own life, if you are asking about the definition of suicide. (*Suicidium* is Latin for "taking one's own life.") While we all share responsibility for Jesus' death, it was the Jewish leaders who organized his execution, and the Romans who technically carried out the act of his murder (actually a judicial homicide).

To give one's life for another is not a sin. It is one of the most commendable and laudable acts one could possibly do (1 John 3:16).

6. Cremation

"What does the Bible say about cremation? What is your opinion on it?"

The Bible does not give any position at all on this subject, and I personally have no problem with cremation. In many cultures, corpses are routinely burned. In most, they are buried. In some, they are intentionally exposed to the elements, allowing the birds to peck away the flesh until only a skeleton remains. Some people request that their ashes be scattered over rivers, mountains or special places. In other words, there is no consensus on how most respectfully to dispose of the bodies of the departed.

Many believers, however, are uncomfortable with cremation because they believe such a practice might interfere with our resurrection at the last day. The Bible does, after all, mention a *bodily* resurrection—even though our new bodies are "spiritual" according to Paul in 1 Corinthians 15:44, they are bodies nonetheless. You can see why many believers are uncomfortable with cremation.

My view is that, if God is able to reconstitute the bodies of the dead (in whatever form they may be found in their new and altered state), surely he can accomplish this whether the body is drowned (Exodus 15:4), buried in the sand (Exodus 2:12), dismembered (Judges 20:6), eaten by animals (2 Kings 9:36–37), eaten by humans (Lamentations 4:10) or consumed by fire (Joshua 7:25; 1 Samuel 31:12; 1 Kings 16:18; 2 Kings 23:20; Amos 2:1, 6:10; 2 Peter 3:10–13). For nothing is impossible with God (Luke 1:37). Moreover, it is not intuitively obvious that we are honoring God more with our bodies in a moldering, decomposing state than in an incinerated one.

In the final analysis, given the silence of the Bible, the cremation issue will need to remain an opinion matter.

7. 'The Kenites'

"I recently studied with someone who has been influenced by the teachings of a man who preaches that Satan impregnated Eve. He also claims that Cain was the result of that illicit union and that Cain's descendants, the Kenites, survived the flood and are around now. I showed him Genesis 4:1–2, 7:21–23 and Judges 1:15–17. Any suggestions on how to proceed?"

Outlandish speculations will always flourish whenever one smooth-talking teacher can acquire an audience—and their money—as prophesied in 2 Peter 2:1–3. The Bible urges us to not pay attention to zany doctrines (Hebrews 13:9; Colossians 2:4, 8). Still, I will offer a couple of thoughts:

- If Satan is a fallen angel, as is commonly held, then as a sexless being, he may well be incapable of procreation (Matthew 22:30).
- The Bible clearly states that Cain was born as a result of Adam's impregnating Eve (Genesis 4:1), not through Satan's seed.
- Satan's "offspring" are not his physical seed, but his spiritual seed (John 8:44).
- While the Bible hints that the Nephilim may have survived the flood (Genesis 6:4), nowhere

does it suggest that the Kenites—mentioned in Numbers, Judges, 1 Samuel, 1 Chronicles, and Genesis (chapter 15 only, after the flood)—were descended from the line of Cain (Genesis 4).

8. Death Penalty

"Should Christians support the death penalty for those who commit murder? After all, isn't it wrong to kill people for killing?"

This is a complex question, though a good one. Many Bible readers point to Genesis 9:6, insisting, "See, God demands the death penalty here." Yet while the New Testament recognizes that the governments of man may enforce capital punishment (see Romans 13:4), it is difficult to build a NT doctrine on an OT law. Though I am wary of supporting the death penalty—because of inconsistency and slowness of application, not to mention the irrevocability of a wrong decision—I am afraid this may need to remain a matter of opinion.

I would, however, like to point out a major inconsistency among proponents of the death penalty. The same OT law that stipulates execution for murder also requires execution for adultery. But who favors that? Certainly not most death penalty advocates. The Old Testament required the death penalty for many crimes and offenses. Following is a list of capital crimes I have found in the Old Testament. (Some lists might be longer or shorter, though substantially the same.)

1. Adultery (Leviticus 20:11)
2. Attacking one's parents (Exodus 21:15)
3. Bestiality (Exodus 22:19, Leviticus 20:15)
4. Blasphemy (Leviticus 24:16)
5. Bull goring (Exodus 21:29)
6. Contempt of court (Deuteronomy 17:12)
7. Cursing parents (Exodus 21:17, Leviticus 20:9)
8. Being a rebellious, disobedient son (Deuteronomy 21:20–21)

9. [Female] promiscuity (Deuteronomy 22:21)
10. Idolatry (Exodus 22:20; Deuteronomy 13:5, 17:2–5)
11. Incest (Leviticus 20:11–12, 14)
12. Kidnapping (Exodus 21:16, Deuteronomy 24:7)
13. Being a malicious witness in a capital case (Deuteronomy 19:16–21)
14. Manslaughter (Genesis 9:6, Exodus 21:12, Leviticus 24:17, Numbers 35:16–21)
15. Priestly arrogation (Numbers 3:10, 18:7)
16. Sabbath breaking (Numbers 15:32–35)
17. Sodomy (Leviticus 20:13)
18. Sorcery (Exodus 22:18, Leviticus 20:27)

Do you see the difficulty here? Where do we draw the line? Why favor a death penalty for murder (based on the OT law), while rejecting a death penalty for other capital crimes in OT law? The position we assume must be *consistent*—both internally consistent and consistent with the letter and spirit of the Scriptures.

9. Islam

"I'm a former Muslim who is now a disciple of Christ. I recently got into a bit of a theological argument with Muslims, who argued that God does not have a son, and that the Bible has been corrupted. I tried to answer them, but since I was not 'allowed' to use the Bible (they believe it's been changed), I had only my convictions to back me up. I would appreciate any references you could give me on Islam."

Well, you had your convictions backing you up, but also God himself. You have taken a stand in becoming a Christian, and as you are experiencing, this means that there will be some sacrifices. I am proud of you for your determination.

You may not have been "allowed" to use the Bible, but it is possible to use the Qur'an itself in refuting the charge that the Bible has been corrupted! I would like to point you to an article I have written on this subject that should be very helpful to you as a former Muslim.[1] The gist (as you will see) is that Muslims seemingly had no problem with the Christian Scriptures for many centuries; the allegation of corruption came later. And ironically, the Qur'an itself has been changed, edited, suppressed, updated!

I might simply mention to your friends that whereas Mohammed was arguing against the crude pagan concept that gods and goddesses produced children, Christians accept nothing of the kind. Rather, they believe that the Son's relationship with the Father is not one of begetting, but is eternal. (See Geisler and Saleeb, *Answering Islam*.)[2]

10. The Qur'an and Jesus

"What do Muslims think about Jesus? Does the Koran ever refer to him?"

The Qur'an (or Koran), which actually mentions Jesus Christ far more than it does Mohammed, teaches the virgin birth of Christ, as well as his Second Coming, but not his crucifixion. (Muslim apologists call it the cruci-"fiction.") They consider Jesus to have been one of the greatest prophets of all time, though Mohammed, according to all Muslims, is the last and greatest prophet.

Interestingly, Islam was developed nearly six centuries after Christianity started. By this time, the church was worshiping Mary and the saints, engaging in many corrupt practices and persecuting those it disagreed with. The "Christians" whom Mohammed mentions in the Qur'an were in all likelihood far, far from the Spirit of Christ. Mohammed taught that Christians should obey the gospel (*Injil* in Arabic), which he obviously considered them to not be obeying.

Muslims' perception of Christians—whether false Christians or true—has naturally been conditioned by their historical experience of and interactions with them.

11. Ibn and Walad

"Muslims say Allah does not have children. How can I get across to them that we Christians do not believe Allah had children by a wife and that Jesus is not his biological son?"

Muslims do not always use the word "son" in a strictly biological sense—as in Arabic *walad*. There is another word for son, *ibn,* which does not necessarily imply procreation. Moreover, Muslims may speak of Mohammed as "Father of Our Nation." This need not imply the citizens are physically descended from Mohammed. In other words, Muslims are as well able to distinguish between literal and metaphorical meanings of words as anyone else. Their real "beef" with the divinity of Christ is theological.

Among the polytheistic Arabian tribes, against whom Mohammed argued, the local gods were said to have wives (consorts) and children by them. Seventh century Catholicism worshiped Mary as the "Mother of God" because she was the mother of Jesus. It takes little imagination to see why Mohammed reacted so strongly against the Christian doctrine. Yet the term "Son of God" never implied Jesus was sired by the Father or that there was a time when he did not exist (John 8:58). Rather, "Son of God" describes analogically the relationship of Jesus Christ to the Father. So tell your Muslim friends, "We agree with you. Jesus is not God's literal, biological son"!

12. Sequel

"Is there going to be a sequel to *The God Who Dared?*"

Thanks for your question. Yes, eventually I do plan to publish the sequel—the outline has even been written for several years. To be honest with you, the appetite of the average disciple for expository books—those which seek to bring the Scriptures to light through careful study—is not very great. As a result, works which cover books of the Bible don't tend to sell as well as other works. My publishers have to pay their employees, so they have to be wise about what to publish and when. I think that when there are many more disciples on the earth, there will be a bigger audience for expository books. In the meantime, thanks for understanding.

The sequel book was to be titled: *The God Who Dared: Genesis from Abraham to Egypt.*

13. Role of the Teacher

"Doug, it seems to me that the role of teacher (*didaskalos*) isn't really an office, but a role that some leaders fill (prophets in Acts 13:1, pastors in Ephesians 4:11 and apostles in 2 Timothy 1:11). Only 1 Corinthians 12:28 lists it separately—and perhaps Romans 12:7. What is your understanding of the role of a teacher? Is it a Biblical office or simply a word describing one who teaches?"

My view, like yours, recognizes that sometimes we seem to be reading a description of a function more than of an office. I suspect that many leadership positions in the early church displayed a similar fluidity, which is why it is often difficult to nail down exactly (and dogmatically) what specific roles entail. I have written at some length on this in chapter 4 of *Life to the Full*—see the excursus on teachers. Perhaps a more practical response on my part would be to provide a list of criteria—really, just suggestions—which I have shared with many brothers and sisters who have asked about the role of the *didaskalos* during the past couple of years. I hope you find it helpful.

1. The teacher must be an excellent student of the Bible. This is the prime criterion! How many times have you read the whole Bible? Do you push yourself? Do you love the Word?

2. The teacher must be ahead of the pack academically. To lead others, he must not be slower than them in his thinking or lagging behind them in his attitude toward learning.

3. A university degree is helpful and highly advisable. Ultimately, I believe the greater the level of responsibility within the teaching ministry, the higher the degree required (e.g., a master's instead of a bachelor's, a doctorate instead of a master's).

4. He must be able to lead a group. Whether a family group, sector, region or church, invaluable lessons are learned through this process. (Note: Not all appointed teachers will serve as church staff members. However, experience on staff does afford a unique perspective on how staff people think. And these are the very people who need most to be moved through the teacher's ministry.)

5. He must enjoy outside reading. The average person in the movement reads only a few books a year. The teacher must have a true appetite for learning. The question for the prospective teacher is not, "How many books do you read a year?" but, "How many books do you read each week?"

6. Knowledge of Greek and Hebrew, while not essential, is desirable. Few persons in the movement read either language—which puts them at a disadvantage when it comes to exegesis of Biblical texts. By far the best way to learn one of these languages is to enroll in a university level course (with intensive study and examinations).

7. His marriage and family need to be exemplary. Just as in the case of evangelists or elders, family qualifies him to do what he does, and family can also disqualify him from doing what he does.

8. His wife must have passion for the ministry as well; they must be well matched in leadership.

9. He must be able to organize his thoughts and put them to paper (Ecclesiastes 12:9–10). Whether writing articles, books, on-line columns or class outlines, the clear thinker will deliver a clear lesson.

10. He must be a reasonably good speaker. Dynamism and authority are essential. His life must back up his message, and he must command the respect of those he seeks to influence.

11. He must have deep convictions and a prophetic commitment to Biblical principles. He must be a man to be reckoned with.

12. Time is required. Training in the teaching ministry, like training in eldership, involves years of work behind the scenes. A young Christian should not be appointed a teacher. Generally the teachers will be persons who have been in the Lord ten to twenty years.

I close these thoughts with my favorite poem by Longfellow:

> The heights by great men reached and kept
>   Were not attained by sudden flight,
> But they, while their companions slept
>   Were toiling upward in the night.

14. Consumerism and Materialism

"I am doing a study on the effects of consumerism in our society. Do you have any reading ideas?"

Indeed I do! I would like to suggest four works in particular. They are good for the soul, and I highly recommend them. May your study bear fruit.

Ronald J. Sider, *Rich Christians Living in an Age of Hunger: A Biblical Study* (IVP, 1977). This is a classic! In fact, when I met my wife-to-be some twenty years ago, she too had her own copy. I think that this little volume, along with the Bible, deeply influenced us as a couple. It affected our spending habits and patterns and is a big reason we have been able to avoid debt.

I credited *Rich Christians* in the book I wrote with Douglas Arthur, *I Was Hungry!* (Boston Church of Christ, 1987). Twenty thousand of these little volumes were given away to the fledgling movement in 1987, urging organized outreach to the poor and needy.

Sider has also written *Living Like Jesus: Eleven Essentials for Growing a Genuine Faith* (Baker, 1996). Once again, his original *Rich Christians* will make you think. It was written "to disturb the comfortable."

Charles Sheldon, *In His Steps: "What Would Jesus Do?"* (Smithmark, 1992). This stirring story will move your heart. These days the "WWJD" acronym has become very popular. Read *In His Steps* to understand the background to a popular religious slogan. Easy reading, yet definitely worth it.

Craig L. Blomberg, *Neither Poverty nor Riches: A Biblical Theology of Material Possessions* (Eerdmans, 1999). This is a scholarly work. The theology is solid, and I would highly recommend it to the serious student. We must be careful not to swing to ultraradical erroneous conclusions, despite how well they might preach or how comforting they might be in light of our lifestyles.

Robert Wuthnow, *Poor Richard's Principle: Recovering the American Dream Through the Moral Dimension of Work, Business & Money* (Princeton University Press, 1996). One of the most helpful sociological works I have ever read, this is a penetrating analysis of the true values of American culture, which is rife with consumerism.

This book informed and influenced my book *The Spirit.* (See especially chapter 14, "The Spirit of the West: The Curse of Consumerism.") In my opinion, consumerism is a real threat to the momentum and unity of the movement of disciples worldwide. Jesus too was concerned with the threat of materialism. This is especially clear in the Gospel of Luke (the Parable of the Sower, the Parable of the Rich Fool, the Rich Man and Lazarus and many other passages).

I believe Wuthnow's *Poor Richard's Principle* should be required reading for any business executive and for all evangelists and preachers.

15. Cubits

"What is a cubit?"

The cubit was a common OT measure of length. Although scholars are still discussing its exact length, it likely originated as the length of a man's forearm, from the elbow (Latin: *cubitum*) to the tip of his middle finger. It seems the "common cubit" was eighteen inches, or a foot and a half (about 46 cm). Thus the ark, at 300 cubits in length, was 450 feet, or 300 x 1.5 x 12 x 2.54 ≈137 meters long. The "royal cubit" was twenty inches (51 cm), while the "long cubit" measured twenty-two inches (56 cm). In general, to go from cubits to feet, just multiply by 1.5. To convert roughly to meters, divide by 2.

16. The Didache

"I recently read the Didache, which is described as a handbook for the early Christians. I was curious as to why it didn't make the final cut, in terms of being canonized along with the other books of the Bible. After reading it, I didn't necessarily see anything heretical written in it or anything out of the ordinary. A lot of the sayings could be traced back to the Bible. So what happened?"

Most scholars assign the Didache a date in the first or second century, and certainly much of it reflects the purity of earliest Christianity. There are several elements, though, which are at variance with Biblical teaching—either by contradicting it or by going beyond what is written in the New Testament. It did not "make the cut" because it is not apostolic—written by an apostle or under the supervision of the apostles. Personally, I find it to be interesting reading, though I would like to stress that nothing from the subapostolic period, the time immediately following the time of the apostles, is authoritative for us as disciples.

Didache, by the way, is pronounced "did-ah-KAY" and is simply Greek for "teaching."

17. Literacy in the Time of Jesus

"Could most people write and read in the first century? Was Jesus teaching the illiterate masses, or were many of them able to read and write?"

Despite many tightly held opinions about the "illiteracy" of the society in which Jesus ministered during his years on earth, the evidence paints quite a different picture. While not everyone who could read could necessarily write, a huge percentage of the free population *had* to read signs, inscriptions on coins, census material and of course, tax information, bills and receipts. The archaeological evidence is overwhelming. Yes, professionals were often employed to write—even the learned Paul used a secretary—but this should not be taken to prove the ignorance or illiteracy of the population at large.

For more on this fascinating subject see *Reading and Writing in the Time of Jesus*.[3] This excellent book contains eight fact-filled chapters, solidly researched: (1) Ancient Books and their Survival, (2) Early Christian Manuscripts, (3) The Form of the Book: Page Versus Roll, (4) Writing in Herodian Palestine, (5) A Polyglot Society, (6) Who Read and Who Wrote? (7) Oral Tradition or Written Reports? and (8) Writing and the Gospels.

Palestine in the first century, though Aramaic speaking, was well familiar with Greek and Hebrew—not to mention the little bit of Latin that some of the Roman soldiers and politicians must have known. It is fair to describe this society as trilingual. (How about you?)

18. Evidences Web Sites

"What are some useful Web sites I can visit on Christian evidences?"

There are many, many useful Web sites out there. While some are sloppy or claim more than the evidence really warrants, most are helpful and reliable in what they present. Once you find a good Web site, look for links to other sites—just as you would check the bibliography of a good book for further reading. Let me suggest just a couple of sites run by personal friends of mine:

- www.Doesgodexist.org (Run by John Clayton.)
- www.Evidenceforchristianity.org (Operated by John Oakes.)
- www.Acesonline.org (Operated by Mike Taliaferro and the Johannesburg crew. This site has material on archaeology [Steve Kinnard], science [John Oakes], and other Biblical evidence [Jacoby].)
- In addition, I have greatly enjoyed the evidences work of Ravi Zacharias (www.Rzim.org) and Hugh Ross (www.reasons.org).

19. Dinosaurs

"Where are the dinosaurs mentioned in the Bible? How would you answer this question, and what scriptures convey the truth about the matter?"

The fact is, nowhere in the Bible are dinosaurs mentioned! Nor are quasars, black holes, blue-green algae or DNA. The Bible is a book focused on humans and our relationship with God. It does not focus on a million interesting facts of science and history. God has taught us much through history and through science—where "natural revelation" speaks to all persons with the ears, instruments and patience to listen. No, the Bible is given to us for a specific purpose. It is not filled with details unintelligible to hundreds of generations of readers.

Some persons mistakenly assume that the end of Job is speaking about some sort of dinosaur. Yet the crocodile, here described poetically (nonliterally) as a fire-breathing monster, is not a dinosaur. No one I have spoken to takes the passage one hundred percent literally.

Others reason that if land creatures and humans were both created on the sixth day, taking this day literally, then they must have co-existed (à la *The Flintstones*). Geologically, this is highly problematic. Odder still is that no humans in recorded history, including Biblical history, ever described their encounters with dinosaurs. I think it is doubtful they lived at the same time, and provisionally I accept the 65–67 million-year buffer between dinosaur and human existence, as the biologists have been teaching. It is not essential, after all, to take the six creation days literally, and there are a number of reasons not to construe it this way. (For more on this, see my book on Genesis and science, *The God Who Dared*.)

Dino-fever may never abate. It was all the rage in the mid-1800s, especially shortly after Darwin published *The Origin of Species*. It was rampant when I was a little boy in the 1960s. My own children too succumbed to the mystery and the infatuation. (Sounds like maybe you have, too!)

20. Hippocratic Oath

"Wasn't there once a pledge doctors used to have to make about not performing abortions?"

Yes, indeed! Please listen to the words of Hippocrates, the great ancient Greek physician (died 377 BC). The following is the "Hippocratic Oath"—once required of doctors to recite in this form. (I have edited it for clarity and relevance to your question.)

> I swear by Apollo the physician…that, according to my ability and judgment, I will keep this Oath and this covenant. To reckon him who taught me this Art equally dear to me as my parents, to share my substance with him, and relieve his necessities if required; to look upon his offspring on the same footing as my own brothers, and to teach them this Art, if they shall wish to learn it, without fee or stipulation; and that by precept, lecture, and every other mode of instruction, I will impart a knowledge of the Art to my own sons, and those of my teachers, and to disciples who have signed the covenant and have taken an oath according to the law of medicine, but no one else.
>
> I will follow that system of regimen which, according to my ability and judgment, I consider for the benefit of my patients, and abstain from whatever is deleterious and mischievous. I will give no deadly medicine to anyone if asked, nor suggest any such counsel; and in like manner I will not give to a woman an abortive remedy….

Whatever, in connection with my professional practice, or not in connection with it, I see or hear, in the life of men, which ought not to be spoken of abroad, I will not divulge, as reckoning that all such should be kept secret.

While I continue to keep this Oath unviolated, may it be granted to me to enjoy life and practice of the Art, respected by all men, in all times. But should I trespass and violate this Oath, may the reverse be my lot.

What do you notice about the oath? A number of things strike me. Not to counsel naivety, still I urge us as a society to consider how far we have wandered since the days of the fourth century BC physician.

- No tuition fees for medical school!
- No euthanasia. (Sorry, Doctor K.)
- No abortion.
- No breach of confidentiality.
- A curse is invoked on any physician who reneges on his pledge.

21. Pagans

"Could you clarify how ancient races outside the Middle East had the opportunity to learn about God? For example, what about the aboriginal culture of Australia, which is more than forty thousand years old, or the Pacific islanders or the Aztecs?"

Without the Scriptures or the Hebrew prophets (who addressed a number of Middle Eastern nations), the Gentiles had the opportunity to learn about God only through nature (Romans 1:18–20, Acts 14:16–17), conscience (Romans 2:9–16) and their experience of following or violating God's universal moral law (Romans 1:32). Yet this should not be taken to mean that ancient races could be saved by works, by being decent persons or by reaching some minimal standard of God-consciousness. The Scriptures are clear that all have fallen short of the glory of God (Romans 3:23). As Romans 2:12 puts it, "All who sin apart from the law will also perish apart from the law, and all who sin under the law will be judged by the law."

Naturally, God is the Judge, and he will make the final decisions, but the Biblical pattern indicates that the Lord brings people into relationship with him through a covenant. I am not aware of any covenant that extended to the aborigines of Australia, the Aztecs or anyone else. What I do know from my study of ancient cultures and civilizations is that they were characterized by sin as much as we are today, including ritual prostitution and human sacrifice. Though they are often glorified by liberal sociologists, anthropologists and artists, I do not buy the argument that primitive peoples were especially closer to "nature and goodness" than we are. Rather, as Paul stated, "*All* have sinned and fallen short" (Romans 3:23, emphasis added).

22. Politics

"What is your opinion on whether it is right for a Christian to be involved in politics?"

I am very wary of politics. (Maybe this is because we live in the Washington DC area!) Certainly, it is in part because I have studied what happened to the church when it started playing the political game, especially in the fourth century. At the start of the century, the fires of persecution were hot, keeping the church relatively purified. Then in 313 AD the state decreed an end to persecution. By 325 the non-Christian Roman Emperor was telling church leaders how to run the church. And by 381 "Christianity," which was increasingly corrupt, became the official religion of the Empire. You would think that with the powerful Roman Empire on your side, you would have nothing to lose. The lure of the world and politics blinded the eyes of Christian leadership, and the church in effect sold its soul to the state, only partially recovering from its declension at the time of the Reformation, some 1200 years later.

On the individual level, I think it is rarely good for a disciple—especially for his family, if he or she has one—to plunge into the world of politics. A couple of years ago I was studying the Bible with a friend of a (recent) former

U.S. president. His observation was that the higher up you go, the more corrupt things are. While the majority of persons who enter politics do so from good motives, he explained, after years of climbing the political ladder, the percentage of good motives falls off drastically. He guessed that perhaps only ten or twenty percent of politicians retain their integrity—and not one at the higher levels. As Lord Acton said, "Power corrupts. Absolute power corrupts absolutely."

In other words, politics is a world of temptation for the soul (the greed; the money; the "favors" expected; the multitude of mutually exclusive obligations that push one to dissemble and evade the issues, instead of embracing them).

This is not to say that *no* disciple should *ever* enter politics, only that few ought to attempt it, and even then they must beware. After all, if politics was the way God wanted us to change the world, why is it that Jesus Christ never proceeded down the perilous corridors of politics?

Let me close by relaying the historical observation of a well-known Biblical commentator. Commenting on Isaiah 31:1–3 and the strong temptation of eighth century BC Israel to trust in political alliances to solve their problems—instead of relying on God—the Jewish scholar Abraham Heschel wrote:

> Isaiah could not accept politics as a solution, since politics itself, with its arrogance and disregard of justice, was a problem. When mankind is, as we would say, spiritually sick, something more radical than political sagacity is needed to solve the problem of security. For the moment a clever alignment of states may be of help. In the long run, it is bound to prove futile.[4]

Summing up:

- Politics were not the way of our Lord. While he did not forbid us from entering politics, he repeatedly warned us about true leadership, which is spiritual and humble (see Mark 10:45).
- Politics fatally ensnared the church in the fourth century and presents pitfalls for us as well.

- Politics would place soul-damaging pressures on most of us. The rewards would rarely be worth the hazard.
- The "higher up" one goes in politics, the more one is expected—even forced—to compromise.
- To end on a positive note, 1 Timothy 2:1–2 enjoins us all to pray for our political leaders. (Do not bad-mouth them, slander or gossip about them, or in other ways be unsupportive. Their job is hard enough.)

23. Traffic Regulations

"The Bible says we are to obey the law of the land, its authorities and their rules (1 Peter 2:13–17, Romans 13:1–7, Titus 3:1). If going against laws instituted by the government is sin, wouldn't this include breaking traffic laws? I break traffic laws every day. Maybe if I have always disobeyed the traffic laws, then I never was a disciple."

A disciple is a learner. That's what the word means. The fact that you are earnestly asking this question indicates that in spirit you are a disciple. So, to begin with, let's not question our salvation just because we are unclear about how to obey the thousands of laws that have been legislated in our country (or in any country, for that matter).

Yet, it is true that Peter's and Paul's passages on obeying the authorities implicitly enjoin obedience to laws. Some laws are simply stupid to disobey: Parking in a tow zone, and paying upward of $100 to get your car back; driving 80 mph in a 55 mph zone; or endangering others' lives by running a red light or passing on the inside lane. Some traffic laws, however, are baffling to me! I find myself, probably once every month or two, not being able to figure out what a sign is intended to get across. I have been to college, so I reckon that if I am struggling with this, probably most other drivers are confused, too. In cases like this, I try to guess what's right and be consistent.

I want to obey the law—so I won't fear the authorities—but there is a certain latitude we as citizens take in our understanding of the law. This is actually unavoidable.

Now I don't know which traffic laws you are breaking every day. If you mean you are driving 70 mph in a 65 mph zone, I probably wouldn't sweat it. (Though I realize there are some disciples who would take issue with me.) But if you mean that you are dealing with your own road rage, jumping of red lights and parking where you please, no offense, but I consider you a menace to society and a nuisance to me. Of course civil disobedience necessitated by conscience or Biblical principle is a totally different matter to careless disobedience of clear safety regulations. But that is not what you asked about, otherwise we would be examining Daniel 6.

I read somewhere that the United States has literally tens of thousands of laws. The Old Testament has 613. The New Testament has just "the law of Christ" (Galatians 6:2), which itself consists of a few simple precepts. So, let's keep it simple. As a disciple, you shouldn't be breaking traffic laws every day. Repent! But obedience to the law of the land is not the highest good you can fulfill in your life.

Whatever you decide on these sometimes tricky matters, make sure you are not judgmental toward others who may not share your opinions (Romans 14–15). Drive safe; arrive alive!

24. Horoscopes

"I would like to ask you about your attitude toward horoscopes. Can they ever be useful for knowing a man's character and using this knowledge for better communication—even to determine marriage compatibility?"

The Bible speaks against astrology in a couple of passages (see Isaiah 47:13) and for good reason. Not only is astrology associated with idolatry, but it is based on illogic. Your "fortune," they say, is determined by the sign under which you were born—that is, your luck depends on your birth date.

But individual existence surely precedes actual birth date! (How do the stars know whether you are still *in utero* or have already been delivered?)

Moreover, distant stars have virtually no gravitational or magnetic effect on our bodies. In fact, computer screens have far more physical pull on you than any constellation in the heavens! There is a slight gravitational attraction between objects in the room where you are sitting and your body—millions of times more influential than the effect of, say, the planet Mars or the constellation Leo.

Finally, horoscopes are impossibly general. What is said about the Scorpio could equally well apply to the Pisces or the Taurus. There is a simple reason for this: the more specific these pseudoscientific prophecies, the more often they are seen to be nonsensical. Those whose incomes are bound up with the gullible public's belief in horoscopes are not likely to risk their own fame and fortune by moving out of the realm of the vague.

So, actually, I do not think horoscopes are useful for anything—other than for a good laugh! Marry freely—any "sign" of the twelve will do. As long as a marriage is spiritual in its foundation, it will succeed.

25. Eloping

"The Bible talks a lot about sexual immorality being a sin. What is your take on an engaged couple studying the Bible, seeing they are living in sin, then eloping in order not to have to worry about their relationship being immoral? What passages could you share with me on this subject? Is this okay in the eyes of God, or is there a deeper heart issue?"

I think a couple who pulls this kind of stunt is likely to have major problems down the road. Separation, self-control, patience—these are what make for a harmonious and God-focused relationship down the road. While the Bible doesn't talk about eloping, it does recognize any legal marriage (between two unmarried persons of the opposite sex—thought I'd better clarify that!) as a valid marriage.

On the other hand, once the couple marries, they are technically no longer living in sin—better married than shacking up! Yet the secretiveness of eloping indicates a pattern of mistrust and independence that will need to be broken if the couple are ever going to form a stable family.

A better approach in certain situations might be to upgrade the relationship to a legal marriage through a visit to a justice of the peace. Later, after the two have become Christians, a larger wedding celebration could be held to allow friends and family to share in the double joy—the joy of salvation as well as the joy of marriage. In any case, this is one arena of life where "many advisers make victory sure" (Proverbs 11:14).

26. Miraculous Gifts

"I was surprised to read that writers such as Origen, Justin Martyr and Irenaeus reported examples of 'miraculous gifts' as late as the second and third centuries. Is this related to the precanonization of the New Testament? Do you think these writings are more reliable than modern miracle accounts? If so, how does this dovetail with the view that apostles were the 'passers' of the gifts?"

The perspective of the early church—let me define "early church" as believers during the first century after Pentecost—seems to be that the supernatural gifts (not the natural gifts) eventually faded out. Justin was writing at a later time, while Irenaeus and Origen are better known as third century writers. Sometime in the second century, the growing "cult of martyrs" permeated the church. Moreover, heretical groups often claimed miraculous power to legitimize their churches. To describe this as an increasingly superstitious age is putting it mildly!

In other words, I do not necessarily accept the "signs and wonders" of the later second and third centuries as authentic. As for the New Testament, though it is not the case that all congregations necessarily possessed every

New Testament document by the close of the second century, certainly by this time the entire New Testament corpus had been written and widely distributed. So, I doubt that the reported "miracles" of the period you are referring to have anything to do with the canonization of Scripture. For more on the subject, see *The Spirit*.

27. Gambling

"What is the Biblical teaching on gambling?"

Before I share some thoughts about this topic, let me "fess up" that I myself recently gambled. A group of friends was watching the Superbowl, and they asked me to join in a game and put down $5.00. There was one chance to win per quarter of the game and the amount wagered was small, so after initially insisting "I am not a gambling man," I eventually gave in—and ended up winning $33.00. Was this wrong?

The Bible has little, if anything, to say about gambling—directly, anyway. But it has a great deal to say on stewardship, and it is my opinion that for the most part, gambling is poor stewardship. For example, the lottery—one of many get-rich-quick schemes—promises enormous pay-outs to the winners, yet chances of winning approach the infinitesimal. Maybe one person wins, but millions lose—especially the poor, the elderly and minorities, those who most often play the game. I personally do not want to have anything to do with this, though another Christian's conscience might allow him or her to participate. (If you personally have a problem with this, let me encourage you to read Romans 14 and 15.)[5]

But back to stewardship. God is not a cheapskate. In Mark 14, see Jesus' reaction to those who criticized the woman for wasting the expensive perfume on him. Yet on the other hand, he does hold us accountable for our thoughts, words and actions (Psalm 19:14, Matthew 12:36, 2 Corinthians 5:10, Hebrews 4:13). Many parables show that the Lord expects wisdom in our use of money and possessions (see Luke 10:25–37, 12:13–21, 16:1–15, 18:18–29).

You will need to determine the truth about gambling from your convictions based on God's word, as well as from your experience and your own conscience. In nearly all instances, I would think that gambling is a poor choice and not the will of God. It leads to loss of self-control and financial ruin; nor is it any secret that organized gambling has historically attracted organized crime and prostitution.

Yet there are degrees of "gambling," of taking various risks. For instance, would it be irresponsible for a man who makes $100,000,000 a year to buy a raffle ticket? (Are you sure?) So let's not be too judgmental, but rather, strive to speak only where the Bible speaks.

28. The Apostle James

"I was wondering about the apostle James. Jesus spent his most important times with the three—James, Peter and John. We know Peter was chosen as the apostle to the Jews and John went on to live the longest and write five books of the Bible. But as for James, he was the first to die, and we never hear much about him in the book of Acts. As disciples, we usually give the best training to those who are able to use it. I have heard it taught that Jesus did not go after large crowds, but focused the heart of his teaching on a select few who would then go out and preach the message. If this is true, why would James be the first to die, as it was so early in the movement? What are your thoughts on this?"

My thought is that Jesus himself had a very short public ministry, perhaps three or four years. James' ministry was longer than that of Jesus, yet Jesus himself made an enormous impact before dying young. It's a matter of quality, not quantity. With twelve apostles in training, the loss of James was a heavy blow, but not an insuperable one.

29. Biblical Greek and Hebrew

"Do you have any book or dictionary recommendations for those of us crazy enough to want to learn Biblical Hebrew and Greek?"

The best advice I can give is this: study the Biblical languages in a university language class. To master any language—especially an ancient one!—structure and accountability are needed. By this I mean classes, quizzes and exams. I am afraid that otherwise, "half-learning" is the best you will do—which is worse than knowing nothing. Someone said, "A little learning is a dang'rous thing; drink deep, or touch not the Pierian spring." Of course there are teach-yourself books you can buy, and these may serve as a helpful introduction, provided they are followed up with college-level instruction.

30. Jesus' Profession

"How can we be sure that Jesus was a carpenter?"

Jesus was the eldest son of Joseph, husband of Mary. Joseph was a *tekton*—a woodworker or master craftsman. (We get our word *architect* from the Greek *arch* [chief] + *tekton*.) Though never explicitly stated in the Bible, it is reasonable to assume from the question asked about Jesus in Mark 6:3—"Isn't this the carpenter?"—that Jesus was a professional craftsman, too.

31. When Was Jesus Born?

"Was Jesus born in the year 0? I guess the BC-AD thing means he was, but I have never read the actual date in the Bible. Also, I am wondering what year he was killed. Can you help me?"

Seven hundred years before Jesus was born, Isaiah prophesied his birth, life and sacrificial death in great detail (Isaiah 7, 9, 11, 53, etc.). Copies of Isaiah have survived from 200 BC and are on display in the Israel Museum in Jerusalem. Yet the OT prophecies never specified the exact year. Christ was most likely born in Bethlehem around 7–5 BC. (Herod the Great, who tried to kill him, died in 4 BC.) This fulfilled the prophecy of Micah 5:2, many centuries earlier. Our calendar, which was created in the Middle Ages and is based on several chronological errors, has Jesus being born before his true birthday! Keep in mind also that there is no "year zero." Conventionally BC means "before Christ," but AD means *Anno Domini*— Latin for "in the year of our Lord." This is why there is no year zero.

Jesus began his public ministry when he was "about thirty" (Luke 3:23), probably in 27 AD, based on the chronology of Luke 2 and 3. He ministered in an area of about ten thousand square miles, similar in size to Massachusetts, the seventh smallest U.S. state. In other words, he ministered to a region far smaller than one percent of one percent of the planet—but what an impact!

As for his death, Jesus was likely crucified in May of the year 30 AD, in his mid-thirties. Crucifixion was never inflicted on Roman citizens (except in cases of treason). It was more common as a method of execution for slaves, revolutionaries and hardened criminals.

32. Language of Jesus and the Apostles

"What language did Jesus and the apostles speak? I hear that the New Testament was written in Greek. Was this their native language?"

Actually, the question should be not "what language," but "which languages." In Galilee, which is the northern part of Israel, not only were Aramaic and Hebrew spoken in the first century, but also Greek. It is very likely that Jesus was trilingual. Their native tongue, at least the one they would have felt most comfortable speaking, was probably Aramaic—a language still spoken today in some quarters.

33. Jesus' Family

"I am wondering how big Jesus' family was. I know he had brothers. Did he have sisters?"

According to the New Testament, Jesus came from a family of at least ten (Matthew 13:55–56). This passage names his four brothers, and then mentions "all his sisters." This phrase implies he had at least three, doesn't it? So here's how I figure the tally at ten:

Jesus = 1
His four brothers = 4
His sisters = 3+
Joseph and Mary = 2
Total = 10+

I am aware that millions of churchgoers believe Mary bore only one child, Jesus. They teach that it would have somehow compromised her holiness if she had ever had sexual relations with a man. Yet the plain teaching of the Bible is that Mary had many other children. In fact, the doctrine of the "perpetual virginity" of Mary is actually shattered in the very first chapter of the New Testament (Matthew 1:25)!

34. Satan an Angel

"Was Satan formerly an angel? I have heard people mention this numerous times, but I can't find a scripture that directly supports this. If he wasn't an angel, where did he come from?"

You are right; there is no scripture which directly says that Satan was an angel. The commonly cited Isaiah 14:12 may shed light on the matter, but in context it is referring to the king of Babylon, as the chapter explicitly states. (The same could be said of Ezekiel 28.) So where did Satan come from?

God created him, since God is the Creator of all. And since everything God created was good—at least to begin with!—Satan must have been good once. But he changed; he rebelled. And apparently other spiritual powers followed him. The traditional, Roman Catholic understanding must be pretty close to the truth. And yes—he "masquerades as an angel of light" (2 Corinthians 11:14). "Masquerade" doesn't necessarily mean he isn't an angel, only that he isn't an angel of light. He is in fact the angel of darkness.

35. Satan's Bible Study

"How did Satan learn the Scriptures? We say 'even Satan knew the Bible' when he tempted Jesus by misusing the Scriptures. How did he learn them to begin with?"

This question invites my utter speculation! Satan's interest in the Scriptures is not spiritual, but solely for the purpose of turning others away from his archenemy, who is our Lord and Savior. I don't think that when we say, "Satan knows the Bible," we mean to say that he has it all committed to memory or that he understands every passage. Far from it! In fact, Satan quotes very little scripture in the Word itself. Yet since his aim is to get us to leave God, to reject his sovereign reign in our lives, it is to Satan's advantage to interfere with our Biblical understanding. How might he do that?

He might persuade us to neglect reading at all. (Few disciples are sucked in by this tactic.)

He might convince us that our opinions are not worth reexamining. (We end up reading to find confirmation of what we already believe.)

He might tell us that we don't need to "interpret" the Bible, that all passages are clear and "mean what they say." (This approach makes lazy students of us all. After all, everyone interprets or comes to an understanding of what a passage is saying. And none of us is an infallible interpreter.)

He might diabolically lead us to doubt God's word. Instead of our faith getting stronger the more we read, we get more questions and qualms that pop into our heads.

He might allow us to read fully and deeply, but entice us to keep our beliefs to ourselves if they are not "spiritually correct" or they don't match up to what our ministry leaders say. Thus we end up thinking one thing while living another—a sort of Orwellian "doublethink." He might allow us to be drawn to those who twist the Scriptures—false Christians or false prophets. See 2 Peter 2:1–3, 3:16. If we are content to let them do our thinking for us, we are vulnerable, liable to be blown about by "every wind of teaching."

36. Who Was Caesar?

"Who was Caesar? And why was a salad named after him?"

The original Caesar was Julius Caesar—the great Roman soldier, statesman and author of the first century BC. His nephew, Octavian, later changed his own name to Caesar Augustus. (*Augustus* in Latin means "majestic or venerable.") It seems that from this time onward, Roman emperors favored the title Caesar. So, there was not technically *one* "Caesar"; there were many. As for the salad, this is what I found on the Internet:

> A salad consisting of greens (classically, romaine lettuce) tossed with a garlic vinaigrette dressing (made with Worcestershire sauce and lemon juice), grated Parmesan cheese, croutons, a coddled egg and sometimes anchovies. It is said to have been created in 1924 by Italian chef Caesar Cardini, who owned a restaurant in Tijuana, Mexico.[6]

To return from Mexico to Rome…Caesar Augustus was emperor when Jesus was born, just as Tiberius was the Caesar when Jesus was crucified. Following is a list of Caesars and their dates from the beginning of the Roman Empire to the time of Constantine, when church and state contracted their fatal marriage alliance. Each man has an interesting story, and there is no shortage of books about these leaders of what was once the most powerful empire on earth.[7]

Caesars Through the Ages

Augustus 27 BC–14 AD	Caracalla 211–217
Tiberius 14–37 AD	Macrinus 217
Caligula 37–41	Elagabalus 218–222
Claudius 41–54	Alexander Severus 222–235
Nero 54–68	Maximinus Thrax 235–238
Galba 69	Gordian III 238–244
Otto 69	Philip 244–249
Vitellius 69	Decius 249–251
Vespasian 69–79	Gallus 251
Titus 79–81	Valerian/Gallienus 253–260
Domitian 81–96	Gallienus 260–268
Nerva 96–98	Claudius II 268–270
Trajan 98–117	Aurelian 270–275
Hadrian 117–138	Probus 276–282
Antoninus Pius 138–161	Carus 282
Marcus Aurelius 161–180	Diocletian 284–286
Commodus 180–192	Diocletian & Maximian 286–305
Pertinax 192	Constantius & Galerius 305
Septimus Severus 193–211	Constantine 306–337

37. America and Ancient Rome

"I have heard that Western culture, especially American, is paralleling the ancient Roman Empire in many ways and is on the way to destruction. Do you have any comment on this?"

Yes, I do. The West—usually referring to European and North American culture (and also to that of places like Australia and the Republic of South Africa)—may not be falling politically or militarily (yet), but certainly it has begun to fall morally. According to Edward Gibbon (1737–1794), author of *The Decline and Fall of the Roman Empire,* there were five signs which characterized Rome as she was deteriorating from within. (Note, the Roman Empire officially "fell" in 476 AD.) The signs were:

1. increasing love of show and luxury (affluence)
2. widening gap between the very rich and the very poor
3. obsession with sex
4. freakishness in the arts, masquerading as originality
5. increased desire to be supported by the government

How uncanny! Not surprisingly, many social critics have drawn the parallel between ancient Rome and modern Western culture. Since America leads the world in resources and affluence, she is an apt choice for the comparison.

38. CE and BCE

"What are CE and BCE?"

In an effort not to offend those who are uncomfortable with the claims of Christ, many persons, in academic circles especially, prefer the abbreviations CE (Common Era) and BCE (Before the Common Era) over the traditional BC (before Christ) and AD (*Anno Domini,* Latin for "in the year of the Lord"). The era is presumably "common" because the entire world, even those who are not Christian, have the same calendar in common. So, CE and BCE are the politically correct forms of AD and BC. Actually, in certain parts of the world the year is uniform only as far as international relations, commerce and computers are concerned, since various people follow different calendrical systems according to their religion. Judaism and Islam are two notable examples. Yet whether the abbreviation is changed or not, the number for the year (for example, 2002) is still based on the notion that more than 2000 years ago Jesus Christ was born; God became flesh; the most significant event of all history took place.

39. Dead Sea

"Why or how is the Dead Sea 'dead'?"

The Dead Sea has a phenomenally high salt content—
around thirty percent!—and no life can survive in it. This
is why it is called "dead." Not surprisingly, another name
for this body of water is the Salt Sea.

Incidentally, at its surface, which is approximately 1300
feet below sea level, the Dead Sea is the lowest depres-
sion on the face of the earth.

40. Mount Gerizim

"In John 4:20, what is the place of worship on 'this mountain'?"

The Samaritans built their own temple on Mount Gerizim
as a rival worship center to the Lord's temple in Jerusalem.
This was destroyed in 129 BC by John Hyrcanus, though it
is clear from the Samaritan woman's question that memory
of it was still strong two and a half centuries later.

41. Pelagianism

"Recently, an article I read accused my church of
Pelagianism. From the context, it seems Pelagius believed
that Adam's sin was not passed down, except in the sense
that we imitate his sin. Also, I gather that he taught that
one only receives the Holy Spirit at baptism. The article
said that his teaching was refuted in the fifth century by
the church. Have you read about Pelagius and his teachings? Why (how) did the church at that time refute that? I
have been taught that the original sin doctrine began in
the seventh century to support infant baptism. How does
all this relate? Also, the part about receiving the Holy Spirit
only at baptism bothered him, evidently, because we teach
that you must change without having received the Spirit
(so it is human strength). I can think of several verses that
demand non-Christians to repent, but I was wondering if
you could help me on the historical aspects of the questions. Thanks a lot!"

Since we do not believe one is born damned, many will label us as "Pelagians." So be it! Yet the doctrine of original sin was earlier than the seventh century. Augustine advanced it around 400 AD as an apologetic for infant baptism, a practice then becoming common, which he wanted to legitimize. We believe of course that some changes happen after baptism which could never happen before, due to the indwelling Holy Spirit. It is not true that we deny the work of the Spirit in a person's life before conversion. Even Jesus said that he draws us to God as we seek him (John 6:44). It would take many words to explore the theological implications of Pelagianism, but I do hope these few words help.

42. Jesus' Return

"I've done a study on Jesus' return. Jesus' return is talked about in most of the New Testament books. From what I can tell, the brothers and sisters of the first century were eagerly waiting for his return. Are we sinning if we do not have an eager heart for Jesus to return? Should we be praying daily about this? I've wondered how Jesus might feel about coming back if we weren't asking for him."

I think you are right. Many of the New Testament churches seem to have been living in the expectation of Jesus' imminent return. Yet there are a number of passages that imply the opposite. For example, Ephesians 3 speaks of "all generations," and the Pastoral Epistles discuss building for the long term. Both seem to be valid perspectives: being ready at all times for the return of the Lord *and* preparing for a long winter before the renewal of all things in the glorious blossoming of the new order.

Now should we pray daily for the Lord's return? My sense is that probably we should, though I find it hard to do this in light of the lostness of most of the world. Other disciples I have talked to about this do not have this struggle, but it is hard for me to pray for Jesus to come back *now*. (Later, yes!) I realize that this is my subjective perspective.

To sum up, we need to get ready, stay ready· and get others ready for the great and glorious coming of our Lord.

43. Illegal Aliens

"I am trying to gain a conviction about how I feel about people living illegally in the United States. The Bible says we need to love the aliens and help meet their needs. On the other hand, I know it is technically illegal for a foreigner to live in the United States without a proper visa. As we are meeting and studying the Bible with people whose status is illegal, should we call them to return to their home countries or maybe work with them toward getting their citizenship?"

This is a tricky question. Surely someone's salvation is more important than his or her immigrant status. We are called to obey the laws of the land, and yet our land (for us Americans) is a nation built on immigrants. Inflexible policy or conviction may not necessarily be in harmony with the principle of love. And yet here are some perspectives that may help you to round out your understanding of this complex issue:

- The Bible does indeed call us to love the alien.
- You are right; we should do all we can to move "illegals" toward lawful status in the country.
- In many cases, going back to countries of origin is unrealistic or even dangerous. "Asylum" may be an abused status, but there are thousands of legitimate cases where shelter from religious or political persecution is needed.
- In many cases, going back to the nation of origin is highly desirable, especially when the individual is more likely to understand the gospel in his own language and as he observes it being lived out among compatriots.
- In most nations, we have thriving churches in which returning disciples would flourish spiritually.

- Of all aliens, high-powered nationals should be encouraged to return, as their contribution to the evangelization of their nations will be maximal.
- Lying to immigration authorities can damage one's conscience. Living in fear or being always "on the run" can erode faith. It may be better to come clean, plead for clemency, and let God move in his own way.
- While we must respect governmental authorities, we are never called to be vigilantes who cause trouble or hardship for those who, for whatever reasons, have chosen to "hide" from immigration authorities.
- We must never let false sentimentality lead us to gloss over deeper issues. In other words, if an "illegal" is also failing to repent of laziness or bitterness, we should not excuse these very serious sins because of false guilt. ("We have so much, they have so little, and we 'owe' it to them to tread lightly, not pushing the implications of the gospel.")

Probably the best course of action will need to be decided case by case.

44. Death and the Old Earth Theory

"I understand (and have read) your view of the old earth theory. I was wondering how you would line up the old earth theory with Romans 5:12. It seems that if death were already occurring prior to the fall of man (which would be the case if the earth is billions of years old), then this would violate this passage. What do you say?"

I would say that "death" in Romans 5 refers to death in the *human* realm. (I would also be wary of trying to tie this passage too closely to 8:22ff.) Death must have been a part of God's plan from the very beginning, insofar as there are millions of microscopic organisms whose life and death is integral to human physiological function. In addition, God had already given the plants to man for food; therefore botanical death was authorized *before* the Fall.

45. 120 Years?

"In Genesis 6:3 God says his spirit will not contend with man for more than 120 years. Why then did Noah live to be 950, Sarah 127, Abraham 175?"

Many commentators understand the 120 years as the time remaining between God's lament and the coming of the flood. You will recall that Noah had a good 100 years in which to construct the ark. Moreover, there are many individuals, as you notice, who live well past the age of 120. That is why I do not take the 120 years as any sort of age limit.

46. Codex U

"I would like to know what books Codex U—which is said to be housed in Venice—includes?"

This ninth century manuscript includes the four Gospels only. You will find it in the Biblioteca San Marco in Venice. In 2001, along with a couple of leaders from our church in Munich, I had the opportunity to inspect a similar manuscript in the library of the University of Munich. It too was a Greek manuscript of the four Gospels (missing only a few leaves) dating to around 900 AD. Apparently the last person to read this precious codex before us did so more than ten years earlier! The libraries and museums of the world are often filled with Biblical treasures—unappreciated by most people, yet readily available to Christian students of the old texts and languages—for whom they are a sort of treasure trove!

47. Drinking Alcohol a Sin?

"Is it wrong to drink alcohol, according to the Bible? I have always thought it was fine as long as you did not get drunk, but recently I decided to research it because my father-in-law won't even come to church because of his beliefs about absolutely no alcohol or dancing. A Web site I found cites 1 Timothy 3:2–3—'Now a bishop must be... temperate [*nephalion*]...no drunkard [*me paroinon*]...' It says *nephalion* means 'physical abstinence, especially from wine,' and the phrase *me paroinon* means 'not near or beside wine.' It says this prohibits even moderate drinking for a church leader. If true, would it not imply that no disciple should drink? Please clarify this issue."

Let's begin with the Greek. The Web site, frankly speaking, is wrong. *Nephalios* means "sober" and *paroinos* means "drunken." Whoever "translated" these words (a) has not studied ancient Greek, certainly not in a serious way and (b) is over-interpreting, probably because there is an ax to grind.

Undoubtedly, alcohol consumption has wrecked millions of lives through the course of human history, but so have many things which, *correctly handled,* are benign or even positive in their effects. It would be easy to list many things that fall into this category: electricity, airplanes, painkillers and television come to mind. All can be abused—but this is at best a weak argument for avoiding them.

You are right—drunkenness is never acceptable for any disciple. But consumption of alcoholic beverages, in moderation, is not a sin. Even Jesus was criticized for this! I have studied the arguments on both sides—teetotaling as well as moderation—and respect those who advance the arguments, even if I do not respect all of the arguments themselves.

Passages like Romans 14–15 and 1 Corinthians 8 certainly come to mind. And yet these passages are about causing a brother to *stumble*—possibly falling away from the Lord. They really have no application to the brother who is determined to *grumble*. It is the violation of conscience that is in mind, not the violation of opinion—no matter how tightly held.

48. Joking Around

"I am curious to know if the Bible talks about joking around with one another. I did not see anything on the subject in my concordance. I want to find some scriptures because sometimes I feel we are joking around too much and should get more serious. Do you have any ideas on what to study out?"

Sure, some joking is ruled out for the disciple: for example, "coarse joking" (Ephesians 5:4). But I think maybe you are overanalyzing. There is much in the Bible about encouraging one another—humor makes this a more attainable goal. In addition, there are many Biblical passages and situations that are humorous in the extreme. Much has been written about this—books like *The Humor of Jesus*.[8]

Certainly laying all seriousness aside is a serious problem—but so is its opposite, being so uptight that we never enjoy our salvation. If you want to do a more thorough study on what we should say to one another, one of the best books is Proverbs, which has dozens of passages on wise and foolish uses of the tongue. I suggest you begin there.

49. Star of Bethlehem

"Could it be that Matthew's virgin birth account contains pagan elements? God despises sorcery, divination and witchcraft (Deuteronomy 18:10, 14; Isaiah 2:6, etc.). Those who followed the 'star' were 'from the east' (Matthew 2:1). Why would God work through such an event to signify the birth of his Son?"

I think your suspicion is half right. God revealed himself to pagans, rather than to the "wise men" of the Jews, thus shaming the "chosen people" while presaging his choice of the heathen, to whom the gospel would soon open up and become available. Yet the only elements of the nativity account which are necessarily "pagan" are the pagans themselves. Quite possibly they were astrologers, yet in this case the "stars" led them to truth instead of to error, or to wishful thinking or to the usual objects of their priestcraft. The star—whether it was a comet, as some have suggested, or some other temporary celestial phenomenon—led them to Christ. And as is often quipped at Christmas time, "Wise men still seek him."

50. The Middle East

"What exactly is the 'Middle East'? East with respect to what?"

I will try to answer in as nonconfusing a manner as possible (but beware!). From the perspective of the "Old World," namely Europe before the colonization of the Americas (the "New World") in the fifteenth through the nineteenth centuries, the "East" stretched roughly from Turkey to Japan. In the parlance of the nineteenth century, the "Near East" consisted of the Balkan States of southeastern Europe and the western part of the continent of Asia. The "Far East" referred to those countries bordering the Pacific Ocean and its associated seas, while the "Middle East" would have included such countries as Afghanistan and Pakistan.

Today the term "Near East" is rare, though one occasionally finds it used synonymously with "Middle East." Rather, the term "Middle East" is the common designation for the predominantly Muslim nations of Southwest Asia, such as Saudi Arabia, Iraq and Syria.

One also encounters the terms "occidental" and "oriental." The former refers to the setting of the sun—which as we all know takes place every evening "in the west," while "oriental" refers to the rising of the sun, in the east. The Orient, then, consists of the lands and territories east of the

"Old World," while the Occident, originally referring to the lands of western Europe, now includes the Americas as well. But never mind, the words "occident" and "occidental" have nearly fallen out of usage in the English language, though "orient" and "oriental" have persisted.

Of course, from the perspective of a Canadian or Mexican, Europe is actually "east," while the United States is "south" or "north," respectively. Bottom line, it's all a matter of perspective.

51. Altar to an Unknown God?

"In Acts 17 Paul says he found an altar to an unknown god. Has this altar ever been found? Have archeologists discovered it anywhere in Athens?"

A number of such altars have been discovered in the ancient Greco-Roman world—at least one in Athens itself. Paul takes as the starting place for his evangelism an object recognized by his listeners. We too should move from the familiar to the less familiar as we strive to bring our friends to knowledge of God and his word.

52. Every Nation

"Acts 2 says that Jews from every nation under heaven were in Jerusalem the day the church started. When I count the nations, I see that only a handful are mentioned. Were there others present that we do not know about?"

In Acts 2, Luke is recording the presence of Jews from around the Mediterranean world who had made the pilgrimage to Jerusalem for Pentecost (Feast of Weeks), as the Old Testament required (Exodus 34:22–23). I believe Luke is painting a picture: this was a very international group! (And the picture is substantially accurate, though only twelve or fifteen actual nations can be accounted for.) "Every nation under heaven" is a figure of speech, like "all over the world." If a fellow said, "I have traveled all over the world," this doesn't necessarily mean he has visited every country or had traversed every square mile of the earth's land area. Rather, it underscores the relative breadth of his travels; it paints a picture. So it is in Acts 2.

The use of universal language to describe limited activities or phenomena is well attested Biblically. For example, Genesis 41:57 reads, "And all the countries came to Egypt to buy grain from Joseph, because the famine was severe in all the world." Does this mean that famine was suffered in South America, forcing the denizens of this southern continent to cross the ocean to visit Egypt? Hardly! The phrase "all the countries" suggests that (1) the distribution of grain was no small operation, (2) those who came to purchase grain arrived from a number of directions and places, (3) it was felt that the nations were converging on Egypt (with Joseph as Vizier) to relieve their famine and (4) God was bringing the Gentiles to his people, just as he would later intimate in such passages as Zechariah 8:23.

Let me mention one other passage frequently misunderstood. Colossians 1:6 says, "All over the world this gospel is bearing fruit and growing," while 1:23 states that the gospel "has been proclaimed to every creature under heaven." Does Paul really mean us to take this literally? If so, why in chapter 4 does he urge us to continue sharing our faith? No, the historical evidence shows that although the apostles and the generation that followed them did succeed in evangelizing the Mediterranean world and the continent of Asia as far as India, much of the world still lay unevangelized: southern Africa, Scandinavia, Australia and the Americas, for example. The gospel apparently did not reach China until the fourth century. It took nine and a half centuries before any form of Christianity reached Moscow, though southern Russia was partially evangelized in the first century. "Every creature under heaven" is a figure of speech and nothing more. (See also Deuteronomy 2:25.) "Every nation under heaven," as in Acts 2:5, is another figure of speech.

As students of the Bible, all of us must develop greater sensitivity to the literary forms of the Bible. To fail to do so is to disrespect the Holy Spirit who inspires the word of God (divine revelation) through the words of man (human language). We must not allow the zeal to preach—the desire to attribute colossal success to the early church—lead to coloring our interpretation of Biblical passages or ignoring the historical record.

Notes

[1] See www.Acesonline.org, "The Bible on Trial," under week 5 of the archived material.

[2] Norman Geisler and Abdul Saleeb, *Answering Islam: The Crescent in Light of the Cross* (Grand Rapids: Baker Books, 1993).

[3] Alan Millard, *Reading and Writing in the Time of Jesus* (Sheffield Academic Press, 2000).

[4] Abraham Heschel, *The Prophets* (Peabody, Mass.: Hendrickson, 1962), 73.

[5] Also, you will find some excellent material in *Decision Making and the Will of God* by Garry Friesen (Sisters, Oregon: Multnomah Press, 1999) in the chapter "When Christians Differ."

[6] From the Web site http://food.epicurious.com/run/fooddictionary/browse?entry_id=7278.

[7] The dates get messy because of occasional overlapping reigns or regencies.

[8] Earl F. Palmer, *The Humor of Jesus: Sources of Laughter in the Bible* (Regent College: 2001).

5
Essays

1
The Origins of Christmas

One of my readers asked the following question:

> "Where did Christmas come from? A friend of mine told me it is a pagan holiday, and that Christians should not celebrate it. What do you think about this?"

I wrote the following article in 1986. I believe it will give you the basics about the pagan origins of Christmas.

The Man Who Came in from the Cold

I remember the night. It was chilly, even for Florida, and Dad had a fire burning in the hearth. Even as a seven-year-old, I realized that this spelled certain doom for the jolly man who later that night would squeeze down the chimney. I mustered the courage to ask Dad, "Is there really a Santa?" I was devastated. Doubts soon began to flood my mind as to the existence of "the Stork," the Easter Bunny, even of God himself. In later years I learned that Santa Claus—alias Father Christmas, Saint Martin, der Weihnachtsmann, Père Noël—was merely a corruption of Saint Nicholas, the fourth century bishop of Myra (now in Turkey) who was known for his charity to the poor.[1] His attributes—red suit, reindeer and residence at the North Pole—derive from a blend of pagan legends with traditions about the saints.

December 25

When was Jesus born? Does anyone really know? Early Christians were unsure. Cyprian thought March 28, Clement of Alexandria guessed May 20, Hippolytus supposed June 2. If these early Christian writers (third century), who lived close to the time of Christ, had to guess the date of his birth, how is it that we know better?

Furthermore, according to Luke 2:8, the shepherds were "living out in the fields nearby, keeping watch over their flocks at night."

But what is Israel like in late December, the time traditionally assigned to "Christmas"? It is cold. It is the rainy season (Ezra 10:9, 13; Song of Songs 2:11). The shepherds would *not* be found dwelling in the fields in the winter season and certainly not at night. It is therefore unlikely that Jesus was born after October.

Roman History

Why was December 25 chosen as Jesus' birthday? In 274 AD the Emperor Aurelian, influenced by the Persian cult of Mithras, designated December 25 as the "birthday" of the sun god, *Sol Invictus* ("the invincible sun"). In Mithraic tradition, the deity was born December 25 and celebrated for twelve days. Does this sound familiar? In some circles, worship of the *sun* became identified with worship of the *Son* (see Malachi 4:2).

Then in 354, Liberius of Rome ordered that Christmas be celebrated. This was popular among the Roman people, who had already been celebrating the *Saturnalia* (in honor of *Saturnus,* the god of seed and sowing, December 17–24) as well as the *Brumalia* (from *Bruma,* meaning "winter solstice," December 25)—times of merrymaking and exchanging presents. Houses were decorated with greenery and festal lights. Gifts were given to children and the poor. Yes, Christmas has pagan origins. On top of all this, it is not even the actual birthday of Christ!

Teutonic History

As with the Romans, the Teutonic peoples too had their celebrations of the winter solstice (known as *yule*). The idea was that the sun god was dying or dead, and there were certain things one should do to assist him on his way, thus speeding the recovery of the world from its winter torpor. As the days lengthened around December 22, there was great rejoicing and partying. Thousands of years of Teutonic history make their contribution to the customs of Christmas, and these customs spread with the people into Central Europe, Gaul and Britain.

At the Yuletide, special cakes were consumed, Yule logs were burnt as an incentive to the waxing sun, and fir trees were adorned with lights in honor of the tree spirits. Special greetings and gifts were exchanged, many went a-wassailing, and of course there was the mistletoe, under which one stood and began (only a kiss, mind you) the headlong rush into a night of pagan revelry (see 1 Peter 4:3). Remember that all of this was going on long *before* Christ was born.

Shopping Sprees

What would Christmas be without the frenzied shopping that characterizes our society? Listen to Libanius, a fourth century Roman writer, as he describes the scene in pre-Christian Rome:

> Everywhere may be seen...well-laden tables.... The impulse to spend seizes everyone. He who through the whole year has taken pleasure in saving...becomes suddenly extravagant...a stream of presents pours itself out on all sides.

Yes, Christmas "spirit," often sustained by big business to sell merchandise, is nothing new. Rather, it is an ancient and time-honored tradition.

Closing Considerations

We have seen that "Christmas" is essentially one hundred percent tradition—and non-Christian at that! Yet traditions are condemned in the Bible only if they directly contradict the word of God (Mark 7:6–8). Jesus commanded us to remember his death, yet there is no harm in commemorating his entrance into the world. As one of the few who understands the true origins of this holiday, you can now enjoy the season in a more enlightened manner. So be of good cheer, and Happy Christmas!

Notes

[1] "Saint Nicholas"—patron saint of seafarers, scholars, bankers, pawnbrokers, jurists, brewers, coopers, travelers, perfumers, unmarried girls, brides, robbers and especially children—was venerated by Dutch settlers in North America. Known in their language as "Sinter Klaus," he eventually became the Santa Claus we know today. A feast day in his honor is celebrated on December 6.

2
The Origins of Easter

One of my readers asked the following question:

> "Where does Easter come from? Should Christians celebrate it?"

I wrote the following article in 1986 for *A Light to London*, the bulletin of the London Church of Christ.

Bunnies and Eggs

"Bunnies do lay eggs!" Or so I reasoned as a five-year-old. After all, the legendary rabbit had visited our home that night, depositing a pile of brightly colored eggs. Why he hid them, I did not know. Why some were plain, like ordinary chicken eggs, while others were made of delicious chocolate, was a mystery. And as to how all this tied in to Easter church services, I was clueless. But those eggs—where else could they have come from if the Easter Bunny hadn't laid them?

I was totally confused! And today's religious world is in a most confused state, particularly the part professing to be Christian. What about Easter—with its colored eggs, sunrise services, pageants and parades, hot cross buns and invisible rabbits? Is this high holy day of Christianity Bible-based or just a bit of fun on the level of Halloween? If Jesus Christ was crucified on a Friday, as most scholars maintain, and rose on "Easter Sunday," is there anything wrong with commemorating his resurrection from the dead?

If you are like me, you have been confused over the true origins of Easter. You may not have drawn the conclusion that bunnies lay eggs, but you may have accepted on faith a number of things that are Biblically groundless (1 Corinthians 4:6).

Christian Commemoration?

The Christian church appears not to have celebrated Easter until the second century, according to the witness of early tradition and church history. In fact, there is no Biblical command to observe Easter. Acts 12:4 in the King James Version uses the word "Easter," but this clear mistranslation is corrected to "Passover" in every modern translation, including the New King James Version. "Easter" comes from the name of a pagan goddess, *Eostre*, who was worshiped at the vernal equinox; the term is derived from heathen religion. Like Christmas, Easter is a blend of pagan superstitions and semi-Christian concepts.

Historically, the major problem with observing Easter has been the double standard in commitment that it reinforces. If some days are holy or special, then others are not. And if observing one day as holy means we are giving God less than our best on the other days, we are violating Jesus' command for every true disciple to "take up his cross daily" (Luke 9:23). Paul too warned of the dangers of "occasional" commitment in Galatians 4:8–11. He confronts the kind of thinking that reasons, "If I attend the special service, even though I often miss 'regular' Sundays, I will be acceptable to God—since one Easter or Christmas is worth at least twenty-five 'regular' Sundays!" This double standard leads to lukewarmness and hypocrisy. This is not to say it is a sin to treat some days as more special than others (Romans 14:5–6), yet we must beware of the pitfall of double-standard commitment so prevalent in our religious world today.

Pagan Playground

"Easter" (*Eostre*) is the English spelling of the ancient Assyrian goddess Ishtar, the fertility goddess and consort of Baal, who repeatedly led ancient Israel into idolatry and immorality. In Babylon her worshipers observed a forty-day period comparable to Lent prior to their "Easter," and numerous other pagan religions observed a similar "Lenten" period. Lent, in other words, is a pagan practice absorbed into Christianity. For example, dyed eggs were sacred Easter offerings in ancient Egyptian temples. Naturally, the egg is a symbol of fertility, and ties in closely with sun worship, a practice condemned by the prophet Ezekiel (Ezekiel 8:15–18). Worshipers met the rising sun god at daybreak. And in the ancient Mediterranean world, the pagan cult of Cybele commemorated the death and resurrection of their god annually—

at Easter, of course. In short, the special features of the Easter season are nearly all borrowed from idolatrous religion.

Burn the Bunny?

Should we burn the Easter Bunny, smash the colored eggs, disappoint our children by abandoning the Easter egg hunt and pray for the parades to be rained into the ground? Some would say yes. My position is that these practices are not necessarily harmful, and in our day they do no more to honor the old pagan gods or religions than using pagan names for days of the week honors the sun, moon, Woden, Saturn or Thor. Once again, the snare of the Easter mentality is the license for lukewarmness; for hundreds of millions of nominal "Christians," Easter and other "special" days become the focus and excuse for worldly living the rest of the year. In short, they have been taken "captive through hollow and deceptive philosophy, which depends on human tradition and the basic principles of the world rather than on Christ" (Colossians 2:8).

He Is Risen!

As long as we are not taken captive by the worldly principles behind Easter so that we compromise our commitment, there is no harm in observing Easter. In fact, Easter can and should be a time of great celebration. Christ the Lord is risen indeed! Make the most of the holiday, honor the Lord and avoid the pitfalls. Welcome, happy morning!

3
Racial Prejudice

It hurts me deeply when prejudice takes place among God's people. Though much rarer than in the world and in worldly churches, which are typically all but segregated, prejudice and racism do rear their ugly heads occasionally even among God's people. If you want to do a serious study on these topics, you have no shortage of material in the Bible itself. For example, Jesus' first sermon in Nazareth (Luke 4:16–27) takes up the very subject. A number of NT documents address issues of unity because of various existing forms of prejudice (Acts, Galatians and Ephesians, for example).

Let me make a few practical suggestions on how to guard your own heart from prejudice. Not all will be applicable to you, but I hope they will strike at the crux of the issue and prove beneficial to you:

- Reach out to all sorts of people, not just those of your own skin color or social class.
- Give sacrificially to meet the needs of the poor, regardless of race.
- Adopt a child from another social class or ethnic background.
- Read a newspaper or newsmagazine regularly, and see the destructive effects of prejudice and racism in our world.
- Make friends with people different from yourself. What does it say about us if all our friends look the same and come from the same background? The church is all about breaking through social barriers.

Finally, let me share with you an essay that Russ Ewell and I co-authored in 1993, which also appears in *The God Who Dared,* in an excursus entitled "The Curse of Ham and Racism."

Prejudice is ugly and widespread, knowing no borders. Yet even more detestable is the use of Biblical authority to justify racism. Through the centuries there have always been those who have used religion to gain their own selfish ends. Scriptures have been wrested from their context and made to support countless creeds of convenience and crass self-interest. And the wounded: they number in the millions, from victims of children's taunts to victims of "ethnic cleansing." They are found in every nation of the world, and despite the common claim of professing Christians that they love their neighbor as themselves, little if anything is done.

Below is an exposé of twisted racist reasoning to help us deal with rationalized ugliness wherever it rears its head.

The Curse of Ham

The Argument

The "curse of Ham" is probably the most common racist argument made from the Bible. Slaveholders and some missionaries taught that Shem, Ham and Japheth represent the races of Whites, Blacks and Asians. The reasoning presumes that Jesus was white, though this is incredible since people in the Near East aren't white. Ham was black, so it is claimed. Genesis 9:18 says that he was the ancestor of the Canaanites, whom God said to annihilate. This obviously leads to genocide, slavery and outright exploitation.

Noah cursed Canaan, Ham's son, for his perversity, which continued in the Canaanite people. And, the false argument goes, the *blacks are still cursed,* which explains their poverty and struggles. The visible mark of the curse is dark skin. This argument has been leveled against Native Americans and other non-White minority groups. In the southern United States the "curse of Ham" argument is still widespread.

As another of many possible examples illustrating the consequences of this unfortunate doctrine, consider the case of the Mormons. Until recently, Mormon leaders taught the inferiority of Blacks. Brigham Young, for example, wrote: "Shall I tell you the law of God in regard to the African race? If the white man who belongs to the chosen seed mixes his blood with the seed of Cain, the penalty, under the law of God, is death on the spot" (*Journal of Discourses,* vol. 10, page 110, 1854–1886). Until June 1978, when a "revelation" came to the current Mormon president, Spencer Kimball, Latter Day Saints barred Blacks from the priesthood, since they were under the "curse of Ham." Bowing to increasing civil rights pressure, the Mormons conveniently received the "revelation" and changed their policy.

Biblical Refutation

Ham had *four* sons mentioned in the Bible:

Cush	Also a nation roughly corresponding to modern Sudan
Mizraim	Ancestor of peoples inclusive of the Philistines (also the Hebrew word for "Egypt")
Put	More obscure group of peoples, probably North African
Canaan	Ancestor of morally degenerate Canaanite tribes

The Hamitic peoples are explicitly said to be descendants of Ham, yes, but the curse applies specifically only to *the Canaanites*—a curse realized intensively during the Israelite conquest of Canaan. Once again, it wasn't *Ham* who was cursed, but *his son,* Canaan. So-called Christians using this passage to justify racism show an appalling prejudice as well as ignorance of the Biblical text.

The "curse of Ham" is *not* a curse on Hamitic peoples, such as Egyptians, but a curse on one part of the Hamitic peoples who, oddly enough, weren't black at all. The curse became reality as the Canaanite nations sank deeper and deeper into apathy, immorality, godlessness and even into child sacrifice. Eventually God commissioned the Israelites to totally remove them from the land.

God is Judge and he has the right to determine how he will carry out his judgments. But we have no such insight, no such right. Most important, there is no connection between Hamites or Canaanites and black Africans. The passage has conveniently been lifted from its context to support racist self-interest.

'Adam' Equals 'White Man'

The Argument

Using wordplay for its position, the "Adam equals White man" argument posits that non-Whites are not human beings. Since "Adam" in Hebrew means both "mankind" and "red," and since Blacks and other races don't generally have pinkish skin, non-Whites are not human beings. They belong to the animal kingdom, yes, but *they have no soul.* Obviously, then, to claim that non-Whites have equal rights with Whites is unreasonable.

Believe it or not, this has long been a stock argument of the Dutch Reformed Church, especially in South Africa. Additional "proof" is claimed in that "Edom," another name for Esau, as well as for the nation of which he is ancestor, means "red, ruddy," and that this is the same word as that for "man."

Biblical Refutation

We're dealing with *two different words* in Hebrew. They have the same consonants (', *d*, *m*) but different vowels (*a*, *a* versus *a*, *o*), and they're listed *separately* in the Hebrew lexicon: (' is a consonant, א or *Aleph.*) The confusion arises because Hebrew words are normally written without vowels.

'adham	man, mankind
'adhamah	ground, from which man was made
'adhom	red, as the skin color of Esau; from an obsolete word meaning "tawny"

As an illustration of our unfamiliarity with Hebrew, take the English words *fever* and *favor.* The consonants are the same (*f*, *v*, *r*), but the vowels are different (*e*, *e* versus *a*, *o*). Are the two words related? No, but if you took out the vowels they could be confused. So it is with the *adham/adhom* confusion.

Along the lines of the thinking above, some people reason that since God created man "in his image," and yet we see human beings of many different physical appearances, only one race was created in the image of God. Colored peoples (Indian, Mongolian, Black, Melanesian, etc.) are thus not truly created in God's image. But the image of God is a *spiritual* image, not a physical one.

His spiritual image includes such aspects as spirituality, moral capacity, forgiveness and abstract reasoning. God is beyond our concept of physical "image" because he is beyond our three-dimensional universe. The misunderstanding shows both prejudice and a failure ever to go beyond a remedial Sunday School theology. Moreover, Jesus, being Semitic, would fail to qualify, since Semites aren't a white race. The reasoning also contradicts Colossians 1:15, which says that Jesus is the image of the invisible God.

Exodus and Conquest

The Argument

A powerful OT motif, the "Exodus and Conquest" argument has been used many times by professing Christians. One example is the colonization of America and Africa by Europeans, who sometimes saw themselves as being led out of the "slavery" of the Old World to the "freedom" of the New World.

Along with the *exodus* and settling in the new, "promised" land comes the *extermination,* if necessary, of the aboriginal peoples, just as God instructed the Israelites to purge Canaan of its sinful inhabitants (Deuteronomy 9).

Biblical Refutation

This doctrine shows a complete misunderstanding of the union of church and state under the old covenant and *the separation of church and state* under the new. The church is a people, a race, a nation; but not a geographical people, an ethnic race or a political nation!

Those who espouse this teaching fall into the same trap of arrogance that God had warned the Israelites about (Deuteronomy 9:4–6), forgetting that this was a limited, one-time commission. For OT Israel, actions against other towns or countries were *not* analogous to the conquest of Canaan, as Deuteronomy 20 clearly teaches.

When extermination is condoned, any lesser crime is also condoned: slavery, torture, physical abuse and denial of other human rights and basic needs. This is vividly familiar to us in the colonization of the Americas: disrespect for the lives of native Americans, confiscation of their lands, frequent massacres and final isolation in reservations. In fact, the tale could be told hundreds of times, illustrated from every continent and repeated every century in one form or another.

In Conclusion

Racism is always inexcusable, and any attempt to rationalize it from the Bible is doomed to fail because God is "the righteous Judge" (2 Timothy 4:8); he is love (1 John 4:8); and with him there is no favoritism (Acts 10:34). This means that we must use the Bible correctly, not just to pacify our "itching ears" (2 Timothy 4:3). Let our conviction be that of the Bible.

> There is neither Jew nor Greek, slave nor free, male nor female, for you are all one in Christ Jesus. (Galatians 3:28)

4
Born Damned?
A Fresh Look at Original Sin

What would you think of a baseball game, to employ an American analogy, in which each player already had two strikes against him—before getting up to hit? No one would wish to play the game. How about a version in which you had *three* strikes against you—before ever swinging the bat?

Does this sound unfair? It is precisely what advocates of "original sin" propose. They believe we bear Adam's sin and his guilt in our body from the point of conception. In my opinion, original sin comes second only to Calvinistic "predestination" in the cruelty of its implications. However, we are not here to discuss whether the doctrine of original sin is fair or not, but whether it is Biblical. After all, we don't always understand God's ways.

We will be assessed on the basis of what we have done while in our physical bodies (2 Corinthians 5:10). Therefore, even if there were such a thing as original sin—done neither by us nor in our bodies—it would be irrelevant to the matter of our justification. Thus the Anglo-Catholic position on original sin is unwarranted. And its companion practice of infant baptism, considered necessary to erase original sin, is likewise unnecessary.

The Early Church

The early church did not believe in original sin. Consider this quotation from Aristeides (*Apologia,* around 150 AD):

> And if any righteous person of their number passes away from the world, they rejoice and give thanks to God...and when a child is born to any one of them, they praise God, and again if it chance to die in its infancy, they praise God mightily, as for one who has passed through the world without sins.

It is clear from this and other historical evidence that the doctrine was a much later development. In fact, it was Augustine (354–430 AD) who first formulated a doctrine of original sin as an apologetic for infant immersion, which was becoming widespread around 400 AD. Although infant baptism became an officially accepted practice at that time, it was not normative until the second millennium.

Furthermore, when Luther, himself an Augustinian monk, thought he had restored the apostolic church, he was in fact only taking the church back to the fifth century. Certainly, this was an enormous improvement over the corrupt state of the church at the start of the sixteenth century. Yet most of the key doctrines of Luther were in fact (false) doctrines culled from Augustine! He did not go back far enough. Children are not "born damned."

Romans 5:12

Romans 5:12 is the classic verse used to support original sin, but it does not teach this doctrine at all.

- The verse only says that sin entered the world through one man. It does not specify the manner whereby sin came to affect the rest of humanity or how it was transmitted to Adam's descendants.
- The verse explicitly states that "death came to all men, because all sinned" (see also Romans 3:23). No one is to die for any sins but his own. The word "because" (*eph ho* [Greek] = *in quo* [Latin]) was interpreted rather differently by Augustine, who read it as "in whom." The weight of scholarship is against this translation, as is the context of Paul's argument in Romans 5.
- Paul's argument (see Romans 5:17), if pursued along classical Augustinian lines, results in the position that, just as all humans sinned in Adam, so all humans are saved in Christ. In other words, the whole world would be redeemed—a "universalist" position that is rarely accepted by advocates of orig-inal sin. Of course, such a view is also inconsistent with other NT teachings on the subject.
- If one argues that man is only "potentially" redeemed in Christ, why not argue that man has only potentially—not actually—sinned in Adam?

Thus we see that Romans 5:12 has been seriously misinterpreted. The doctrine of original sin reads a lot into the passage and goes against the natural flow of Paul's argument.

Other Passages

Another verse held to teach original sin is Psalm 51:5: "Surely I was sinful at birth, sinful from the time my mother conceived me." But a cursory comparison of this passage with parallels in Psalms 22:9, 58:3 and 71:6 shows that it is not meant to be taken literally—unless we think wicked infants literally speak lies from the womb! The Psalms, many of them poetic, teach us about human feelings (like the feeling of utter uncleanness David expresses in Psalm 51) and how to pray. The Psalms are certainly not good primary sources for rigorous doctrinal statements.

What the Bible does teach is that there is a sinful inclination from childhood (Genesis 8:21). But infant baptism in no way removes that inclination—just take a look at children who have undergone this ritual! We must take care to distinguish a sinful inclination from sin itself. Moreover, Ezekiel 18:20 clearly teaches that God does not hold the son accountable or guilty for the sin of the father. The principles of personal accountability and free will apply.

This is not to say Biblical baptism is unimportant. An adult who believes and repents of sin is forgiven at baptism for all the sins that he or she has committed. Baptism removes the guilt of sin we have originated, not the guilt of another's original sin!

Immaculate Conception

One curious corollary of the original sin doctrine is that Christ himself somehow escaped being born sinful via heredity. It was postulated that since Jesus had only one human parent, she must have been without original sin, or else she must not have transferred her original sin to him. Many people mistakenly confuse the "Immaculate Conception" with the virgin birth. Yet the doctrine of the Immaculate Conception states that Mary (not Christ) was conceived without sin, with the result that she had no original sin to pass on to her Jesus.

In 1950 the Vatican extended this logic to claim that Mary's mother (Saint Anna, by tradition) was also "immaculately" conceived. This is an official Catholic doctrine. But why not go the whole way? Why not push the regression back a step further and say that every human descended from Anna was preserved from the stain of original sin—or for that matter that all of mankind was spared?

Final Thoughts

I consider this short essay sufficient to refute the doctrine of original sin. And if original sin is refuted, then the associated doctrine of infant baptism becomes wholly unnecessary. We come to bat with no strikes against us. Of course, we all strike out anyway—through our own sin. But to begin with the disadvantages described by the doctrine of original sin—well, that just wouldn't be cricket.

5
Television

Channel 23 Psalm

The TV is my shepherd, I shall not want.

It makes me to lie down on the sofa. It tempts me away from the faith. It assaults my soul.

It leads me in the paths of sex and violence for the sponsors' sake.

Yea, though I walk in the shadow of Christian responsibilities, there will be no interruption, for the TV is with me. Its cable and remote control, they comfort me.

It prepares a commercial for me in the presence of my worldliness. It anoints my head with humanism and consumerism; my coveting runneth over.

Surely sloth and ignorance shall follow me all the days of my life, and I shall dwell in the house watching TV forever.

—Lutheran Witness, July 1994

The following is an adaptation of a paper written for a Politics class in the course of my doctor of ministry studies at Drew University. It has been shortened and simplified. Though directed to ministry staff, it contains some practical considerations for anyone who is a follower of Christ.

A revolution in our perception of science, technology and the media is in order if we are to "escape the corruption in the world caused by evil desires" (2 Peter 1:4). In a key scripture, Luke 17:1–3, we see that Jesus cared not only about sin, but about the media through which temptations come. We too must be concerned not so much about what is "in the air" (the flying demons of medieval Christianity!), but what is "on the air." The call to re-think how we "view" television is fundamentally a call to think.

Does not our Lord always call us to use our mental faculties to follow the truth wherever it leads?

This is of the essence, because the church in our day seldom questions the social system. We are brought up to "eat everything on our plate," so to speak—to ingest the spirit of our age uncritically. We have elevated the virtue of tolerance above all other values. This is demonic. We are even raised to believe that capitalism and exploitation are of God. The average American knows far more about sports than current events and cares little for those in the "outside world." This brings me great heartache, and it is not unusual for my congregation to receive an exhortation to stay current with the news, contribute time and money to help those less fortunate and become key players in the drama of redemption as "the salt of the earth" and "light of the world" (Matthew 5:13–14).

Clergymen, symbols of the American system, likewise are socialized not to question. Having drunk deeply of the "system," they have choked down any natural objections or pangs of conscience. Few churches have the mettle to speak against the system or any part of it. The media need to be scrutinized and exposed.

Root of Social Sickness

In order to formulate a strategy, it is first necessary to identify the problem. In the spirit of Mark 5, we must call the demon by name. Consumerism is a great evil. Now I, for one, do derive some benefit from the "system," which comprises production, marketing, purchase and consumption. Yet injustice is implicit in the capitalist system, as anyone who has visited a third-world country will have realized. The burden of guilt, or the convictions sharpened through third-world travel, testify to our complicity in the exploitative system.

In this day and age, television is the primary medium through which consumerism, violence, immorality and general secularization are intensified in our lives—and nearly every American household owns at least one. What are the results of our consumer-driven economy and the nearly universal denominational support it finds? Consider the evidence of social erosion facilitated by the greed that is prevalent in much of big business—or rather in many of the entrepreneurs who direct them.[1]

- Financial shipwreck. Impulse spending, unprincipled and unbudgeted personal finances, credit card "slavery," and staggering personal (and national) debt plague most of us. Many corporations and their cronies powerfully promote such recklessness. Money is one of the most common subjects of marital disputes. To make things worse, we deprive our children of the opportunity to learn from our mistakes by keeping the subject of money "hushed."
- Disintegration of relationships. The basic social unit is being reduced to the individual alone. Alienation is the characteristic symptom when social erosion affects the familial level.
- Disintegration of health. Television has wrought great harm in its contribution toward nicotine addiction, alcoholism, etc. Laziness is in principle condoned as the lives of the "rich and shameless" are paraded on screen. We as a nation are grossly out of shape.
- Ruin of family values. TV eats up precious family time. A 1996 *USA Today* poll found that the average male watches twenty-eight hours of TV per week; some children, to their detriment, watch even more. Even in the International Churches of Christ, whose members are typically extremely involved in church and community events, there is a crisis in relation to TV. A 1997 survey of Washington DC inner-city preteens (ages 9–12) revealed that the average preteen spends two and a half hours a day watching the tube. Not surprisingly, their parents' viewing time was one and a half hours a day! This has been addressed and continues to receive follow-through. We believe that the ones who need the challenge are not so much the youngsters as their parents, who must take seriously the responsibility to protect and nurture their children during these formative years. For example, infidelity and fornication are

depicted on TV as excusable, "natural" courses of action. Dysfunction is increasingly portrayed as normal. The traditional "family," thanks to the media, is gaining negative overtones.

- Pathetic role models. When convicted felons are kids' role models, we are in trouble!
- Erosion of morality. Violence, promiscuity and materialism are highly exalted in the media and are prime agents in our moral decline. This clearly translates into injustice, crime and hedonism.
- Secularization. These days, money is the bottom line. Worth is defined merely as financial worth; humanity is emptied of that which is truly valuable. Jesus noted that the Pharisees loved money, yet he assured us that "what is highly valued among men is detestable in the sight of God" (Luke 16:15).

Sociologists recognize that secularization takes place through three avenues: (1) the media, (2) the technological explosion and (3) the university. Might we not add a fourth: the church? Truly the church has lost its moorings and is now ethically adrift on—yes—a sea of relativity! Here is the problem: it is "politically incorrect" to speak clearly and authoritatively, to give the direction people so desperately need.

Moreover, the secularization process anesthetizes us against the real violence and immorality in the world. I will never forget the horrific scenes of violence in *The Sand Pebbles* and *In Cold Blood*, films I saw as a youngster. These movies deeply affected my conscious as well as, I believe, my subconscious. Nor will I forget the first time I saw nudity on screen—and the (different sort of) violence that that did to me.

Social sickness results from sick values pushed by the media. Many of the corporations that benefit from advertising and consumerism are highly exploitative. Exploitation takes place both in the corporate sphere and in the consumer sphere. It takes two to tango; in this case we, while often participating unrighteously in the first area, are also guilty of complicity in the second. It is now incumbent upon us to "unmask" the purveyors of worldliness.

Behind the Scenes

Having identified the promoters of selfishness through the media, it is now our task to expose them for what they are. As Richard Horsley[2] soberly adjures us, "Fidelity to the gospel lies not in repeating its slogans but in plunging the prevailing idolatries into its corrosive acids."

Television (standard "furniture" in any home) qualifies fully as an agent of economic exploitation, commercial television in particular. Not that I stand against commercial TV! I am commenting only on the processes in play which lead to the corruption of society and spirituality. What are the intentions of those in power (the Gordon Gekkos[3] of our society), as well as those who appear to profit in a hideous sort of symbiotic relationship?

Through such greed-based corporate aggregates as these, the economic exploitation of our congregations and communities is taking place—not to mention the rest of the world, the Third World in particular. The Madison Avenue lie commonly takes the form, "You will be a happier person if you own product x." Moreover, while an image of "caring" is concocted in the boardrooms of self-seeking businesses, we know what is really going on. The values of big business are all too often "maximize profits; the ends justify the means; money is the bottom line; broadcast whatever brings in revenue."

Although there ought to be enormous resistance to the official doctrines of consumerism, there is virtually none. We are rolling over and letting whole generations be indoctrinated. Tragically, the response to advertising consists of little more than "Cool!" or "I want that!" or "I'm willing to spend money I don't have and work overtime to own more things." We have a prophetic mandate, however, to call the victimizer by name. Well, his name is Mammon and he is "senseless, faithless, heartless, ruthless" (Romans 1:31). His spirit indwells nearly all companies, and he appears not to have a conscience. We need to raise the level of consciousness about this.

Violence, degradation of women and the profaning of what is sacred are indignities to which millions are subjected in the public arena. And Hollywood glamorizes and conceals the truth.

Advertisers conceal the awful emptiness of a life whose value consists in possessions alone. Television stations are willing partners in this duplicity. And, odd as it sounds, we are willing partners in our own deception, in our own alienation. The pressure to conform is an overwhelming current for most men and women.

How is it that the naked truth is still too awful to gaze upon without shame? It would seem that we are not yet completely dehumanized or beyond redemption! Through the bold declaration of the gospel, there is hope. In the meantime, however, we all too often prefer escapism to owning up to our own shallowness and mutual manipulation. These are truths with which we must confront our world, starting with our churches.

I realize, of course, that a more direct approach could be taken. One could go straight to the seats of power (big business or the television companies), articulate the concerns of the public over the misuse of the media and possibly use prophetic, dramatic action. This public critique might flout social convention or even law. One could thus demonstrate that the power is not omnipotent. Boycott might also be effective, either of television stations or products and activities promoted through the stations. Yet I am not persuaded that this is the surest way to effect change in this area, in part because so few people realize the nature of the domination by which they are oppressed. Indeed, we have been trained to love what the media offers—and love it dearly.

We will be wise if we begin our exposé where people's hearts are most receptive, personally modeling the principles we espouse so that there is no confusion about the truth. Church—both the assemblies and the ongoing fellowship throughout the week—is the perfect arena for addressing and exposing the sickness of consumerism.

Are the Scriptures silent as to these evils? Far from it! For consumerism, Amos 6 comes immediately to mind. Then there is the Gospel of Luke, with money as a major theme. How about the violence exhibited ever more graphically on the TV screen? Looking up verses mentioning "violence" in the Revised Standard Version, I found eighty-two! Proverbs 3:31 is an excellent example. Passages on sexual sin also abound, like Job 31:1. The Scriptures speak loud and clear. Are we too distracted by the blaring TV to hear them?

Action Steps

We need to remember that we have been called to do more than to critique. Since we stand in relationship with our congregations— let alone the rest of humanity!—let us formulate and follow well thought-out strategies. This is not a matter of goodwill or general good. Victory can be attained only by concentrated attack, along with a willingness to sacrifice. I am not cynical about the future. Glorious triumphs are in reach.

If we can change the way the members of our churches relate to the television, we can, at least in part, free them from the economic oppression and moral decay from which they are suffering. How, practically, can this be accomplished? Here are ten suggestions which can be easily modeled, preached and implemented at the congregational level.

1. Explain why Big Business wants us to watch the programs and commercials they sponsor. This may seem self-evident, but it is amazing how far an occasional reminder will go.

2. Emphasize how much extra time, energy and money there will be if TV viewing is reduced. Advertising increases our consumption. TV ties up valuable time—not just for industrious activity, but also for relationships, especially marriage and parenting relationships. Those who watch a lot of TV tend to be sluggish and "dumpy" in appearance. Suggest alternative recreational activities.

3. Explain how some corporations target kids in their advertising. It has been my experience that the less kids watch TV, the less they say, "Gimme," especially at such times as birthdays and Christmas.

4. Admonish parents to limit their children's viewing hours. For younger children especially, it is easy to simply tell them, "No, not now."

5. Preach against TV addiction and expect the church to change. It is my conviction that churches generally do what preachers expect them to do. If he expects them to change and is (patiently)

willing to follow through, change will come. Pathetic is the preacher who blames the flock before blaming self.

6.   Model it! Restrict your own viewing of TV, focusing mainly on news, some sports and educational programs. Really, the minister about the Master's business will have little time for the "tube."

7.   Limit the number of televisions in a household. This wise decision will go far toward promoting family life. Sell or give away any extra sets.

8.   Make specific suggestions about what to watch and not to watch. We know our geographical areas and the stations that broadcast. The more specific we can be, the better.

9.   Encourage the people to come to their own personal and specific convictions about this issue. Avoid legalism. Preach from such passages as Ephesians 5:3–10 and Philippians 4:8–9.

10.   Follow up instruction with practical financial advice. Many of our people are out of control in personal finances. Help them to see connections between the mores of the domination and their own indebtedness, unhappiness and manipulation. Stress that we all have choices.

Why do most ministers not speak out against the diabolic way in which the media are manipulated to the detriment of their flock and the surrounding society? I believe they fail to speak—even to see—because they have, at the most fundamental level, bought into the system. They claim to be spiritual, yet they are secular. They are afraid to upset their congregations. And their interpretation of Jesus as a limpwristed, pathetic sort of figure who would never stand up to the system is convenient.

Church leaders do not portray Jesus as radical because (1) unwittingly or not, they are conniving at the system; (2) they are thoroughly "indoctrinated" themselves; and, for some reason, (3) they themselves tend to be limpwristed, weak figures (wishy-washy, "holy tone" and often corpulent). And so they take no stand against the media and their corrupting influence. Instead, they themselves blend in, to the point that they are virtually indistinguishable from the surrounding world.

I say "they" because there will be some who decide to speak out. Someone needs to say something. For, as Edmund Burke[4] has said, "the only thing necessary for the triumph of evil is for good men to do nothing." If the minister does not have the conviction to stand up and be counted, who will?

With this thesis in view, I pledge to recommit myself to preach against economic exploitation and stupidity, beginning with my next sermon. After all, disciples of Christ are called to be shakers and movers.

Ever since this study, I have preached consistently about the ills of consumerism and warned my hearers to protect both themselves and their children against the corruption of the world caused by evil desires. I urge you to do the same.

Notes

[1] It is not my intent here to demonize "big business" and label all corporations as greedy and manipulative. Companies are neither good nor bad. The people who run companies can be evil or righteous, greedy or benevolent. Companies hire people, create revenue, invent products and do a lot of good. We must resist the urge to simply blame the "big guys" for the sins we all commit, although the impact of human sin can be magnified when on such a grand scale.

[2] Richard Horsley is a Biblical scholar and professor of religion at the University of Massachusetts.

[3] Gordon Gekko is the character played by Michael Douglas in Oliver Stone's *Wall Street*—he is a ruthless big-time corporate raider, a Wall Street shark.

[4] Edmund Burke was an eighteenth century British political writer and statesman.

6
Christians and Cigarettes

One of my readers asked the following question:

> "What scriptures would you share with someone who is seriously struggling with smoking cigarettes—someone who knows it's not good for you, but needs to be spiritually convicted? Also, will a disciple who smokes go to heaven?"

Although the Bible does not address the subject of smoking directly, there are a number of principles relevant to the discussion. While it is difficult to prove smoking is a "salvation issue," I would certainly strongly discourage it. Smoking weakens us not only physically, but also morally, opening the door for other sins and compromises to enter and take over.

The following is an article I wrote in 1986 (now slightly modified) for *A Light to London,* the bulletin of the London Church of Christ. I hope you find it helpful—feel free to share it with your struggling friend.

Warning: Smoking Can Be Hazardous to Your Salvation

Smoke pours from his nostrils.... (Job 41:20)

And the smoke of their torment rises for ever and ever. (Revelation 14:11)

While the verses above have quite a different meaning in their contexts, it remains a fact that smoking is a serious social problem. In fact, I am writing this just 350 miles from the Lung Cancer Capital of the World—Glasgow, Scotland, according to a recent World Health Organization report. Yet it is not just Glasgow that is belching up thick clouds of cancerous smoke; the nicotine craze has spread over the entire inhabited earth. All of us have friends who are "hooked." The purpose of this article is to offer a practical study on the subject of smoking, one that you will be able to use as you teach your friends God's word.

Smoking Enslaves

Smoking cigarettes, cigars, etc. is enslaving, and it is a principle of God's word that we should not allow ourselves to be enslaved by anything (Romans 6:12–13; 2 Peter 2:19).

Seeking Relief from the Wrong Source

In times of anxiety or stress, a Christian should not turn to a cigarette to find peace—we are to turn to God! (Matthew 11:28–30, Ephesians 5:18, Philippians 4:6–7).

Honor God with Your Body

The Scriptures teach that our physical bodies are not our own and that we are to honor God with our bodies. Clearly this rules out all self-destructive habits (1 Corinthians 6:20; 2 Corinthians 7:1; 1 Thessalonians 5:23).

Bad Example

Cigarette smokers set a terrible example for those they love: friends, relatives, immediate family. Perhaps those who are hurt most are children. (They are hurt not only by the bad example, but also by the inhalation of second-hand smoke.) In London it is not uncommon to see ten- or eleven-year-olds puffing a "fag" (British slang for cigarette). I certainly appreciate having grown up in a home environment where no one smoked. Never underestimate the force of example.

Waste of Money

At $4.00–$5.00 a pack (depending on the region of the world you are in), smoking can be an expensive habit. God expects us to use his money wisely (Matthew 25:14–30).

Professional Hazard

There are many advantages to hiring nonsmokers. Premiums on health, life, accident and fire insurance policies are lower. Cleaning and maintenance costs for office furniture and equipment are reduced. Smokers take fifty percent more sick leave than their non-smoking coworkers. And mortality rates in the peak working years (ages thirty to forty-five) are four to seven times as great for smokers as for nonsmokers. Thus, over a period of five years, an employer can save up to $2000 a year by hiring a nonsmoker instead of a smoker. Moreover, morale has been shown to be significantly higher in smokefree work environments. So, it is no surprise that personnel managers of large U.S. companies, considering candidates of equal qualifications, opt for the nonsmoker fifteen out of sixteen times! (Source: *Toronto Globe and Mail*, 4 October 1986.) For this reason, more and more American and European work environments are now entirely nonsmoking.

Undermines Influence

Considering the importance of influence in reference to our goal of evangelizing the world, we cannot afford to tolerate habits that undercut our ability to win others to Christ. Smoking alienates nonsmokers, the majority of religious people and smokers trying to quit. In the United States, thirty percent of the population smokes, and eighty-seven percent of those who smoke want to quit, according to polls.

Violates Others' Rights

Smoking can at times be a public nuisance. Did you know that one-third of all fire-related deaths are caused by careless smokers? Smoke fouls clothing, irritates the eyes—especially for contact lens wearers—and significantly increases cancer incidence. (The non-smoking spouse of a smoker who consumes twenty cigarettes a day runs a thirty-three percent higher chance of contracting smoke-related cancer.) Jesus clearly taught us to put others first. The principles of Matthew 7:12 (the "Golden Rule") and Philippians 2:4 are more than common courtesy: they are God's will for our lives.

Serious Medical Risk

One-third of all cancer cases are lung cancer, and ninety percent of these are caused by smoking. A smoker's chances of getting cancer are ten times higher than a nonsmoker's, while a pack-a-day smoker's chances are twenty times higher. Sadly, only five percent of cases of lung cancer are curable. Smoking is also known to cause cancer of the bladder, kidney, larynx, mouth, pancreas, pharynx and trachea. Nonsmokers feel better, are more healthy, and live longer than their smoking counterparts. In fact, the annual death rate (for all causes) is fifty-eight percent higher for smokers.

Shorter Life Span

How can we "[make] the most of every opportunity" (Ephesians 5:16, NIV) or "[redeem] the time" (Ephesians 5:16, KJV), when we chop years off the end of our lives? On average, a pack of cigarettes reduces your life expectancy by six hours. Life is a precious gift that we must conserve, cherish and use wisely in the Master's service.

Folly

In the United States, we are warned, "The Surgeon General has determined that smoking causes lung cancer, emphysema and heart disease." In Britain, where smoking is tolerated in more public buildings (even in hospitals until recently!), the warning, somewhat more dilute, brings the same message: "Cigarette smoking can cause cancer and other serious health problems." Testimony of the tobacco lobbies notwithstanding, smoking is lethal. Ignorance may have been an excuse fifty years ago, but not these days. In light of all the evidence, it is folly (Mark 7:22) to smoke.

Addiction

Many people believe that, compared to alcohol or drugs, smoking is not a serious addiction. In fact, in an effort to quit abusing other substances, addicts often switch to nicotine instead—to their destruction. Consider this excerpt from *Some Sat in Darkness:*

Nicotine is among the most dangerous of drugs and among the most addictive. From a spiritual standpoint, more people fall away from God as a result of nicotine addiction than any other addiction. In [the] New York [church], we've known plenty of heroin addicts who have been able to quit heroin, but have been unable to stop smoking. Part of this can be explained by the fact that a smoker goes into withdrawal from nicotine after only twenty minutes. A single shot of heroin can last an addict a whole day, but a smoker begins to feel discomfort and the need to medicate after only twenty minutes.[1]

Drug addiction of any kind causes deep character damage and emotional immaturity. This happens because, rather than feel emotional pain, an addict "medicates" it away, thus missing the intended growth and lessons.[2]

Jesus promises that this life will have plenty of trouble (John 16:33), but that we will never face more than we can handle (1 Corinthians 10:13). When we do get overwhelmed or filled with anxiety, God's plan is for us to go to him in prayer and to be open with others in the fellowship in order to get help (2 Corinthians 1:8–9, James 5:16). Why trust in a puff of smoke to bring you "peace" rather than in the Almighty God? Kick the habit today—and help the people you love to do the same!

Notes

[1] Mike Leatherwood, Brenda Leatherwood, Declan Joyce and Joanne Randall, *Some Sat in Darkness: Spiritual Recovery from Addiction and Codependency* (Billerica, Mass.: Discipleship Publications International, 1991), 27.

[2] If there is a CR (Chemical Recovery) ministry in your local church, smokers would be well advised to take advantage of it, whether they are disciples or are studying to become Christians. If not, they can—along with their disciplers or those studying the Bible with them—read *Some Sat in Darkness* for further help and direction.

7
The Red Heifer Sacrifice

If you have an appetite for something "meaty,"[1] I believe you will enjoy the following study, which investigates the red heifer sacrifice—a relatively obscure feature of the Mosaic Law—and its astounding significance for the crucifixion of Jesus Christ nearly two millennia ago.[2] Unless you have steeped yourself in the Old Testament, you may be struck by the unfamiliarity of many items in this essay, for it weaves together elements of Torah, Mishnah, history, linguistics, the New Testament and early Christian testimony to support its thesis. And just what are we setting out to determine? That for compelling historical, theological and geographical reasons, Jesus was not put to death at the site traditionally ascribed to the crucifixion, but rather on the Mount of Olives.

Moriah: The Place of Sacrifice

Sacrifice is found in nearly every book of the Bible, and this theme binds together all the other themes and plots in Scripture. The place of sacrifice par excellence is Moriah. Often we hear mention of Mount Moriah. In a sense, there is more than one Mount Moriah. Just as the ark came to rest on one of the "mountains of Ararat," rather than on the Mount Ararat (Genesis 8:4), so Abraham was bidden by God to sacrifice his son on one of the mountains in the land of Moriah:

> Then God said, "Take your son, your only son, Isaac, whom you love, and go to the region of Moriah. Sacrifice him there as a burnt offering on one of the mountains I will tell you about." (Genesis 22:2)

Conceivably a number of "Moriahs" exist. Jesus too was sacrificed in the land of Moriah. There are at least ten amazing parallels, by way of foreshadowing, between the sacrifice of Isaac and the sacrifice of Jesus.[3] Therefore, it should come as no surprise that both were "sacrificed" and "received back" on the same mountain. The sacrifice of Christ takes on new meaning when we understand its foreshadowing in the Old Testament. The site of Jesus' execution, like that of Isaac's "sacrifice," is never identified with the Temple Mount, as is the threshing floor of Araunah:

> Then Solomon began to build the temple of the LORD in Jerusalem on Mount Moriah, where the LORD had appeared to his father David. It was on the threshing floor of Araunah the Jebusite, the place provided by David. (2 Chronicles 3:1)

There are, in effect, *two* theologically significant places of sacrifice in the land of Moriah. The Mount of Olives is located on Moriah, and it is probable that both Isaac and Jesus were offered there. The threshing floor at which David stemmed the plague, indeed the very site at which Solomon erected his magnificent temple, were not on the Mount of Olives, but on Moriah. The Mount of Olives we could call "upper" Mount Moriah, the Temple Mount, "lower" Mount Moriah.

The Four Sacrifices

Sacrifice	Location
Sacrifices with a "resurrection"	*Upper Moriah*
Sacrifice of Isaac	A mountain in Moriah
Sacrifice of Jesus	A mountain in Moriah[4]
Sacrifices without a "resurrection"	*Lower Moriah*
Sacrifice to stem plague	Threshing floor of Araunah
Sacrifice of bulls and goats	Solomon's temple

You may be caught off guard by the thought that the Mount of Olives was a place of worship or sacrifice in the Bible. After all, wasn't this a serene place of prayer? Was blood actually shed on this mountain?

According to 2 Samuel 15:32, there was already a significant place of worship on the Mount of Olives some thousand years before Jesus was crucified:

> But David continued up the Mount of Olives, weeping as he went; his head was covered and he was barefoot. All the people with him covered their heads too and were weeping as they went up.
>
> When David arrived at the summit, where people used to worship God, Hushai the Arkite was there to meet him, his robe torn and dust on his head. (2 Samuel 15:30, 32)

The elevated location was already a place of worship and sacrifice. At any rate, the threshing floor of Araunah (2 Samuel 24; 1 Chronicles 21), located on the other side of the Kidron Valley on what would soon become the site of the first temple,[5] was not the only place where reconciliation between man and God took place. What is referred to as "summit" in the above verse can also be translated "head." The Place of the Head, on the Mount of Olives near the road into the city, was also a "holy place." (More on this below.)

The Red Heifer

The sacrifice of the red heifer[6] is commanded in Numbers 19:2. If you are like me, you are probably unfamiliar with this sacrifice commanded by God through Moses:

> The LORD said to Moses and Aaron: "This is a requirement of the law that the Lord has commanded: Tell the Israelites to bring you a red heifer without defect or blemish and that has never been under a yoke. Give it to Eleazar the priest; it is to be taken outside the camp and slaughtered in his presence. Then Eleazar the priest is to take some of its blood on his finger and sprinkle it seven times toward the front of the Tent of Meeting. While he watches, the heifer is to be burned—its hide, flesh, blood and offal. The priest is to take some cedar wood, hyssop and scarlet wool and throw them onto the burning heifer. After that, the

priest must wash his clothes and bathe himself with water. He may then come into the camp, but he will be ceremonially unclean till evening. The man who burns it must also wash his clothes and bathe with water, and he too will be unclean till evening.

"A man who is clean shall gather up the ashes of the heifer and put them in a ceremonially clean place outside the camp. They shall be kept by the Israelite community for use in the water of cleansing; it is for purification from sin. The man who gathers up the ashes of the heifer must also wash his clothes, and he too will be unclean till evening. This will be a lasting ordinance both for the Israelites and for the aliens living among them." (Numbers 19:1–10)

Why did I include the extended citation of Numbers 19? Because the red heifer sacrifice corresponds to the sacrifice of the Messiah.[7] A sanctifying paste was manufactured from the ashes of the heifer to purify the people (pilgrims as well as those on normal sacrificial errands) so that they could approach the house of God.

Please notice that there was "a ceremonially clean place" *outside* the temple precincts which was, in a sense, an extension of the holy temple. The red heifer sacrifice, unlike those offered on the altar of burnt offering, was conducted *outside* the camp. According to Jewish tradition, nine red heifers have been sacrificed since the time of Moses.[8] Also, the Hebrew writer alludes to this remarkable correspondence between the red heifer sacrifice and the sacrificial death of Jesus Christ:

When Christ came as high priest of the good things that are already here, he went through the greater and more perfect tabernacle that is not man-made, that is to say, not a part of this creation. He did not enter by means of the blood of goats and calves; but he entered the Most Holy Place once for all by his own blood, having obtained eternal redemption. The blood of goats and bulls and the ashes of a heifer sprinkled on those who are ceremonially unclean sanctify them so that they are outwardly clean. How much more, then, will the blood of Christ, who through the eternal Spirit offered himself unblemished to God, cleanse our consciences from acts that lead to death, so that we may serve the living God! (Hebrews 9:11–14)

The heifer sacrifice is also alluded to in Hebrews 13. (What other sacrifice could it be?) This was the sacrifice by whose ashes all Jews entering the temple had to be purified. Many early Christians realized the deep symbolism of this sacrifice. Consider the Epistle of Barnabas, written around 100 AD:

Now what type do you think was intended, when he commanded Israel that the men whose sins are complete should offer a heifer, and slaughter and burn it, and then the children should take the ashes and place them in containers, and tie the scarlet wool around a tree (observe again the type of the cross and the scarlet wool), and the hyssop, and then the children should sprinkle the people one by one, in order that they may be purified from their sins? Grasp how plainly he is speaking to you: the calf is Jesus; the sinful men who offer it are those who brought him to the slaughter...(8:1–2)

Let us continue to trace the thought of the Hebrew writer:

We have an altar from which those who minister at the tabernacle have no right to eat.

The high priest carries the blood of animals into the Most Holy Place as a sin offering, but the bodies are burned outside the camp. And so Jesus also suffered outside the city gate to make the people holy through his own blood. Let us, then, go to him outside the camp, bearing the disgrace he bore. (Hebrews 13:10–13)

The implications for our evangelism of going to Jesus "outside the camp" are worthy of many sermons. We leave traditional religion (temple) behind, forging out of the comfort zone into the dark world we are called to serve. We are called not to sit at home, quietly idling away our evenings, but to pour our time into building relationships with those who do not know Christ. However, our special concern for this essay is the altar where the sacrificial bodies were disposed of, the so-called "Miphkad Altar."

The Miphkad Altar

There is substantial evidence in the Old Testament for a location "outside the camp" devoted to the incineration of the bodies of sacrificial animals, the Miphkad Altar[9] (Leviticus 4:12, 6:11).[10] In Hebrews 13 the writer contrasts the holocausts at the temple with those outside—namely, at the Miphkad Altar, mentioned in Numbers, Ezekiel[11] and the Mishnah. Jesus' death is symbolically connected with this altar outside the temple. (Not to say that the crucifixion necessarily took place *at* this altar.) Where were the bodies of the sacrificial victims totally incinerated?

The Miphkad Altar stood 2000 cubits from the temple on the Mount of Olives,[12] and although few Christians today—or Jews, for that matter—realize its true significance, it was arguably the most important of the three altars of the temple. The three were (1) the altar of burnt offering, (2) the incense altar and (3) the Miphkad Altar (technically a *pit*, according to Parah 4:2).

It is certainly not difficult to see how much richer the symbolism and typology of the death of Jesus is if *our* "red heifer sacrifice" was "slaughtered" on the Mount of Olives, in roughly the same location as the *original* red heifer sacrifice. One final comment on the third altar of the temple. The Mishnah says clearly that the priests offering the sacrifice of the red heifer needed to be able to *see* the altar of burnt offering from their vantage point on the Mount of Olives:

> All the [temple] walls were high, save only the eastern wall, because the priest that burns the Heifer and stands on top of the Mount of Olives should be able to look directly into the entrance of the sanctuary when the blood [of the red heifer] is sprinkled. (Middoth 2:4)

Since the Mount of Olives (upper Mount Moriah) is taller than the Temple Mount (lower Mount Moriah), the priests sacrificing at the third altar were able to look down on the Temple Mount and see (over the intentionally lowered wall) the altar of burnt offering. If Jesus' sacrificial death fulfills the sacrifice of the red heifer, as the Hebrew writer and early Christian tradition affirm, then the Son of God was almost certainly crucified on the Mount of Olives.

But a Calf?

Isn't the heifer illustration inaccurate? Is Jesus not our paschal lamb? Yes, Christ is a "lamb," insofar as his blood, like that of the Passover animal,[13] "covers" us. The parallel is noted in 1 Corinthians 5:7. Yet the Passover lamb was not technically a sin offering. Although the people of God were saved by virtue of its blood, the lamb did not in any sense "bear sin."

Wrap-Up

There were four historic sacrifices in the region of Moriah, the fourth being the crucifixion of Jesus Christ, paralleling the "sacrifice" of Isaac. These two both took place on a mountain in the land of Moriah. On lower Mount Moriah David sacrificed to stop a plague which claimed 70,000 lives, and at this exact location Solomon translated the Mosaic tabernacle service into the temple, along with its sacrificial institutions. The red heifer sacrifice, which mirrors the atoning sacrifice of Jesus,[14] was performed on the Mount of Olives, the approximate site of Jesus' death and burial.

The Mount of Olives

Somewhere on the Mount of Olives is likely the spot where Jesus Christ was unjustly executed. That the Mount of Olives is the authentic location is probable for three reasons: (1) This is the site of the Miphkad Altar and the red heifer sacrifice; (2) there are strong political reasons why Jesus would have been publicly slain on the Mount of Olives, along the Roman road into the city; and (3) this site provides the visual vantage point which best facilitates the centurion's observations, according to the Gospel accounts.

Miphkad Altar and Red Heifer Sacrifice

As we have seen, both Torah and Mishnah clearly declare that the "third" altar of the temple was located on the Mount of Olives, and it was here that the heifer was slain. Moreover, as we have seen, there was already a significant site halfway up the Mount of Olives a thousand years before Jesus was crucified (2 Samuel 15:32). Since the heifer sacrifice represents the sacrifice of the Son of God, it is certainly a good possibility that his death took place on upper Mount Moriah.

Politics

Had Pilate crucified Jesus on a major pilgrim route, a road into the city, this would have made a statement—and quite a loud one—to future would-be "kings." In fact, according to the Roman writer Quintillian, "Whenever we crucify the guilty, the most crowded roads are chosen, where the most people can see and be moved by this fear. For penalties relate not so much to retribution as to their exemplary effect."[15]

The Roman road to Jericho followed approximately the same track as the road at the time of David and would have been the perfect location for any public execution, thus making a political statement. Yes, the strategic location of the Mount of Olives, especially in the middle of a major religious holiday, would have maximized the impact of Jesus' execution. Note also that Jesus began his "triumphal entry" at "Bethphage on the Mount of Olives" (Matthew 21:1). Of course Pilate often showed himself capable of considerable political ineptitude during his ten-year tenure as governor of Judea. Consequently, he could have bungled the opportunity to make a spectacle of Jesus' execution. But the strategic location of the eastern site must be taken into account.

Visual Suitability

Apart from the temple courts themselves, only from the Mount of Olives—across the Kidron Valley from the Temple Mount—would anyone have a clear view of the temple curtain, which was torn at Jesus' death and which the Gospels claim the centurion saw. In a sense, the site of the crucifixion depends on the sight of the temple! In Matthew we read:

> And when Jesus had cried out again in a loud voice, he gave up his spirit.
> At that moment the curtain of the temple was torn in two from top to bottom. The earth shook and the rocks split. The tombs broke open and the bodies of many holy people who had died were raised to life. They came out of the tombs, and after Jesus' resurrection they went into the holy city and appeared to many people.
> When the centurion and those with him who were guarding Jesus saw the earthquake and all

that had happened, they were terrified, and exclaimed, "Surely he was the Son of God!" (Matthew 27:50–54)

The east-west dispute will be further addressed in the following section. Suffice it to say that there are more difficulties reconciling the Gospel descriptions[16] of the unusual events attending Jesus' death with the "western" view than with the "eastern."

Wrap-up

The significance of the Mount of Olives *vis-à-vis* Jesus Christ's (1) triumphal entry, (2) Gethsemane prayer, (3) arrest, (4) crucifixion, (5) burial, (6) resurrection and (7) ascension certainly must not be underestimated. All seven of these events took place east of the city, on the Mount of Olives. Moreover, the Via Dolorosa, (the "Sad Road" in Latin) led not westward from the Temple Mount, but eastward.[17]

What About the Western Site?

The traditional location of the crucifixion of Jesus Christ is at the Church of the Holy Sepulchre, just outside the second wall of old Jerusalem. I maintain, however, that the correct site is on the Mount of Olives—in exactly the *opposite* direction from the Temple Mount. The western site is unlikely to lie in the vicinity of the crucifixion of Jesus Christ, for the four reasons below.

Lack of Attestation

If the western Calvary is authentic, why is there no mention of it in records or Christian writings before the fourth century? In fact, the only site holy to Christians before the fourth century seems to have been the Mount of Olives.[18] The lack of attestation presents another difficulty in accepting the traditional location.

Are we really to believe, as Eusebius relates the story of Helena, the mother of Constantine, that this woman found both the true site of the crucifixion *and* the "three crosses" upon her visit to Jerusalem in 326 AD? Remember, the early fourth century, after the legalization of Christianity (313), was an age of superstition, relics, sainthood and increasing inaccuracy in both the gospel story and the claims of adherents to Christendom. Christians during this time freely adopted and subsequently adapted many pagan holidays and sites, bringing them, under a thin sacral veneer, into the mainstream faith.

The site of the Church of the Holy Sepulchre, visited annually by hundreds of thousands of tourists, was actually the location of the pagan temple of Venus, the goddess of love. This edifice was erected by the Emperor Hadrian in the late 130s AD. So the site *was* "sacred"—but not sacred as the place of Jesus' execution. It was sacred to the spirit of paganism! This is another reason that it seems nothing more than superstition to accept the early Catholic legend of the "Holy Sepulchre." In short, it would be naive to accept the traditional site on the word of Constantine's mother or by virtue of the many "miracles" performed there.[19]

Prevailing Winds

The prevailing winds in Jerusalem blow from west to east. That means that the execution of criminals, for hygienic and olfactory reasons, is more likely to have taken place east of the city. Although the traditional Golgotha lay outside the second wall of the city, it is still very close to the city.[20] And, as we have seen, it does not in any way make sense of the red heifer sacrifice or the mysterious Miphkad Altar.

Visual Problem

Matthew 27:50–54, like its parallels in the other Gospels, suggests that the Roman soldier had a view of the temple. The western site, however, is improperly situated for this; it is located on the wrong side of the temple (which faced east). The curtain, roughly 82 x 24 feet in size[21] and facing eastward, would not have been visible (despite its enormous dimensions) from the traditional Calvary. It should be noted that the curtain in question was not that separating the sanctuary from the Holy of Holies, but an *outer* curtain. Hebrews 9:3, referring to the tabernacle, describes the inner curtain between sanctuary and Holy of Holies as "the *second* curtain." (I realize that this line of reasoning is an *implication*, not a *proof*.)

In addition, the tombs are on the eastern side of the Temple Mount, not on the west. From the traditional Calvary there would have been nothing to see![22]

City Planning

One last reason it is unlikely that the fourth century Church of the Holy Sepulchre marks the site of Jesus' crucifixion is that, in the first century, this area of the city was rather built up and hence less likely to have been used as a place of execution.

Wrap-up

In short, there are serious difficulties with the traditional identification of Golgotha.[23] For a number of reasons, it seems more probable the crucifixion took place east of the temple, on the Mount of Olives.[24]

On a Hill, Far Away

Some favoring the western site as the location of the crucifixion are quick to point out that there is a hillside in Jerusalem that somewhat resembles a skull. General Charles Gordon was apparently the first to recognize this in the nineteenth century. The site has been dubbed "Gordon's Calvary." No similar, "skull-like" location has been suggested anywhere on the Mount of Olives. The problem with this is that no one before Gordon ever reported what he saw. For example, fairly detailed sketches of Jerusalem survive from the seventeenth century; none portrays any skull-like hill. Apparently the formation that Gordon identified came about as a result of fairly recent weathering.

The image of a skull certainly preaches better than that of a head, just as the Jolly Roger is more likely to strike terror into the crew of a galleon than a "happy face" will. Yet the translation of the Hebrew *gulgoleth* and the Greek *kranion* ought not to be influenced by our church traditions.

The Greek word *kranion,* meaning "skull" or "head" (Matthew 27:33, Mark 15:22, Luke 23:33, John 19:17), comes from the Homeric Greek *kara,* meaning "head, top or summit." Often *kranion* translates into the Hebrew *gulgoleth,* while *kephale* translates into the Hebrew *ro'sh*—but not always! *Ro'sh* is Hebrew for "head," as in *Ro'sh hashanah,* or Head of the Year (not "skull" of the year). The point is that Golgotha can just as well signify "head" as "skull." Once again, while "skull" is usually a perfectly good translation of *kranion* in the New Testament and in the LXX,[25] the word can equally well be rendered "head." This makes the identification of Golgotha with the "summit" or "head" of 2 Samuel 15:32 much more convincing.[26]

Hebrew, Greek and Latin Words for "Skull" and "Head"

Word	Bible Version	Language	Definition
Skull	English Versions	English	skeleton of the head, head
Gulgoleth	Masoretic Text (OT)	Hebrew	skull,[27] head[28]
Kranion	Septuagint (LXX)	Greek	upper head, skull
Calvaria[29]	Vulgate	Latin	*cerebrum* = skull, temple
Head	English Versions	English	head
Ro'sh	Masoretic Text (OT)	Hebrew	head, top, chief
Kephale	Septuagint (LXX)	Greek	head
Caput[30]	Vulgate	Latin	*calvus* = head

However, the real questions have nothing to do with whether the hill on which Jesus was crucified resembled a skull or not. They are:

- What is the theological significance of Jesus' death?
- What is God trying to teach us?
- Where was this hill located?
- How do these facts inform our understanding of Jesus' crucifixion?

Conclusion

Well, we have gone deeper into the word of God, and hopefully we have been fed with some solid food!

As we have seen, in the New Testament the crucifixion of Jesus is clearly identified with the sacrifice of the red heifer, which took place on the Mount of Olives. This is exciting, for several reasons:

The Word of God Comes to Light

The Old Testament truly opens up as we grasp the typological significance of the crucifixion and all the details surrounding it. This is precisely the sort of "solid food" of which the Bible speaks (Hebrews 5:14). A Bible study such as this can also help us to appreciate the lines of reasoning available to great minds like Paul and Apollos, which they could have used to win Jews to the faith. This kind of exercise is faith building and beneficial for all Christians as they mature in Christ.

The Truth About the Crucifixion Emerges

Simply stated, traditional Christianity is mistaken in its identification of the western site of the Church of the Holy Sepulchre as the location of Jesus' death and resurrection. The site of the temple of Venus should be recognized for what it is. When visiting Jerusalem, by all means do see this ancient building; yet understand that no amount of sincere devotion or veneration can transform the truth. In addition, there will be little need to "compete" with the tour groups travelling down the traditional Via Dolorosa and inside the Church of the Holy Sepulchre, since we recognize that they are well over a kilometer from the true site of the crucifixion—on the Mount of Olives.

Keep Me near the Cross!

Is it surprising that "traditional" Christianity has misconstrued the meaning—and even the location—of Calvary? So much has been lost; so much must be restored. It is my hope that these thoughts will call us back to the cross—not merely the real location of Calvary but, more vitally, its position in our hearts as men and women of God.

Notes

[1] Much of the Christian literature read in the International Churches of Christ, it must be admitted, is "light" reading: it tends to be of a devotional or inspirational nature. As a movement, we are not used to pushing ourselves intellectually. We prefer simple doctrines, neatly packaged, rather than those that engage the intellect and challenge our thinking.

[2] Thanks are due to Steve Johnson of the New York City church and Ory Mazar of Hebrew University for introducing me to this subject and for answering my many questions and initial objections. Thanks also to Dr. Michael Christensen of the Theological School of Drew University for suggestions on the manuscript.

[3] Here are a few parallels: Each sacrifice was an ultimate test of faith; each was the sacrifice of "a son, an only son"; each was the son "whom you love"; the son was a willing victim; he was sacrificed among the mountains of Moriah; the son bore the wood; there was a confident expectation of a return from the dead; the world was blessed spiritually through the sacrifice.

[4] The exact *geographical* correspondence between the mountain (hill) of the crucifixion and the mount on which Isaac was sacrificed is less important than the *theological* correspondence.

[5] Solomon built the temple from 966 to 959 BC (1 Kings 6:1).

[6] A heifer is simply defined as "a young cow that has not had a calf" (Oxford English Dictionary).

[7] Messianic Jewish groups recognize this connection even today. In 1996 a red heifer named "Melody" was born in Israel. Although once plentiful in Palestine, pure red heifers seem to have died out since the destruction of the second temple in 70 AD, and it is rare today to see a red heifer without white or black spots. In truth, Melody was the result of artificial insemination from an anonymous bull in Switzerland. Nonetheless, her appearance caught the attention of ultra-radical Jewish and Christian groups in 1997, who were convinced that this was an omen preliminary to the reestablishment of the temple. This would, of course, mean seizing control of the Temple Mount from Muslim hands. Ironically, the true location of the temple is not even certain. If Dr. Ernest Martin—along with Professor Tabor of UNC—is correct, the actual temple was not located on the site of the *Haram esh-Sharif,* but hundreds of yards south. See Martin's *The Temples of Jerusalem* (Associates for Scriptural Knowledge, 2001). The implications for politics and peace in the Middle East are significant. See, for example, "A Red Heifer, or Not? Rabbi Wonders" in the Kfar Hassidim Journal, *The New York Times,* June 14, 1997.

[8] Parah 3:5.

[9] In 2 Samuel 24:9 and 1 Chronicles 21:5, the census ordered by David, *miphkad,* has etymological reference to "counting." In Nehemiah 3:31 the *miphkad* gate is rendered "The Inspection Gate."

[10] See also Exodus 29:14; Leviticus 8:17, 9:11, 16:27 and Numbers 19:3, 9.

[11] Ezekiel 43:21, rounding off the discussion of the altar, reads: "You are to take the bull for the sin offering and burn it in the designated part of the temple area outside the sanctuary." Notice that part of the temple area is said to lie *outside* the sanctuary.

[12] This distance is a reasonable inference drawn from Numbers 35:5.

[13] Technically, either a lamb *or* a goat could be slaughtered to fulfill the Passover requirements (Exodus 12:5).

[14] Unlike the "sacrifice" of Isaac, which was most emphatically *not* an offering for forgiveness of sins.

[15] Cited in Martin Hengel, *Crucifixion* (Philadelphia: Fortress Press, 1977), 50.

[16] Matthew 27:50–54, Mark 15:38–39, Luke 23:44–47. John is silent as to the events of the earthquake, the tearing of the outer curtain of the temple and the resurrection of the holy men and women who later entered Jerusalem.

[17] Whether by coincidence or divine design, the tribe of Judah, from which Jesus was descended, was ordered to camp *east* of the tabernacle in the time of Moses (Numbers 2:3). East from the presence of God (and of necessity across the Kidron Valley) is the Mount of Olives.

[18] Eusebius has quite a lot to say about it in his *Proof of the Gospel*. The church historian of Caesarea, familiar with Jerusalem and serving at the court of Constantine, expressed surprise that the "tomb" of Jesus was found at the (western) location of a pagan shrine (*The Life of Constantine*, 3:28).

[19] Through visions and dreams, Helena's informants were able to locate not only the authentic site of Jesus' death and burial, but also three crosses, a sponge and reed, and the *titulum* on which the charges against him were written. Are we really so gullible?

[20] A third wall was constructed a number of years after Jesus' crucifixion.

[21] According to Josephus, who provides eyewitness testimony, the curtain was fifty-five cubits long and sixteen cubits wide. Josephus was serving as Governor of Galilee when the war broke out in 66 AD. He defected to the Romans and witnessed the entire destruction of Jerusalem, about which he wrote in his *Jewish War*.

[22] One might counter, "Wasn't the temple occluded by the three-hour period of darkness? How would the centurion be able to see *anything*?" Perhaps the temple was more difficult to make out—whether the sacrificial fires were burning or not (presumably they were). But, according to Matthew 27:48, it assuredly wasn't so dark (*à la* Exodus 10:23) that the sponge could not be lifted correctly to Jesus' mouth.

[23] Nonetheless, attempts to identify a western location for the crucifixion and burial persist. See Joan E. Taylor, "Golgotha: A Reconsideration of the Evidence for the Sites of Jesus' Crucifixion and Burial," in *New Testament Studies* (April 1998), Vol. 44, No.2, 180–203, and Thomas K. Grose, "Unearthing the Secrets of a Sacred Place: Is the Tomb of Jesus Really the Tomb of Jesus?" *U.S. News and World Report*, No.46, 11/9/98.

[24] For more background on the Mount of Olives, see Zechariah 14:4, which is interpreted eschatologically by many Bible believers. I see its fulfillment, however, in events of the first century AD.

[25] LXX is a designation for the Septuagint, the Greek translation of the Hebrew Old Testament. It was translated in the third century BC, presumably for the benefit of Jews who no longer retained a command of Hebrew. LXX means "seventy" in Roman numerals, corresponding to the supposed number of translators.

[26] Interestingly, the LXX translates the Hebrew *ro'sh* in 2 Samuel 15:32 as, *Rosh*—a mere transliteration. This implies that the "head" was in fact called by that name, and the translators did not want to confuse the reader with a strict translation. (It would be as though we referred to LA as *The Angels* instead of by its better known name, Los Angeles.)

[27] In Judges 9:53, *gulgoleth* is literally "cranium."

[28] In Exodus 16:16, as in 1 Chronicles 10:10, the Greek translation of *gulgoleth* is *kephale*, not *kranion*. These translations are found in the LXX. And in Numbers 1:2, the phrase *la-gulgoleth* (Vulgate *per singula capita* = head by head) translates to [an omer] "apiece" or "per person."

[29] For example, in 2 Kings 9:35 *kranion* = *calvaria*.

[30] Latin *caput* and Greek *kephale* are clearly related to the Sanskrit *kapalam* = "skull"; the fluidity of terms across languages suggests some semantic latitude.

8.
Putting 'Supper' Back in the Lord's Supper

This essay aims to address one of the basics of the faith: our *communion*. People have often asked such questions as why we celebrate the communion only on Sunday, whether visitors should take part and whether forgiveness of sins is somehow directly tied with receiving the bread and the wine. Yet there is another question to consider: Are we sure we are right when we partake of "tokens" instead of an actual meal? Are we really doing as Jesus requested, or do we need to rethink our position?

This essay suggests a return to the original Christian practice of a communion *meal*.[1] It is not intended to answer every possible question, only to bring up the question and suggest a format for meaningful discussion from this point on.

Coming to Terms

Each of the several names for communion tells us something of the nature of the meal.

- *Communion* is the most common term and emphasizes the body life of the church: life in the body of the Lord as well as life in the body of believers. The *common* meal we participate in shows that the fellowship of the body of Christ transcends ethnic, social, racial, linguistic and other barriers

- *The Lord's Supper* (1 Corinthians 11:20) suggests a focus on Christ, the command of Christ to celebrate this meal and the continuity with Jesus' own Last Supper. The natural understanding of the *Lord's Supper* is a meal, as opposed to a snack or token representation.

- *Eucharist* (1 Corinthians 10:16) comes from the Greek word for "thanksgiving" and stresses the attitude every disciple should strive to maintain—gratitude to the Lord for salvation. This term is especially common in high church circles.
- *Love feast* (Jude 12) was another term for communion. Ancient religions often celebrated meals in honor of their gods, and their feasting often led to carousing. By contrast, the Christian meal accentuated the Lordship of Jesus and was a visible and concrete expression of the awesome love of God, as well as of the tough love that binds all true Christians together.
- *The breaking of bread* (Acts 20:7) is another synonym. As Jesus' physical body was broken, so the bread of the communion is physically broken and shared. We all eat of the one loaf. This term underscores the sacrifice of Jesus as well as our common dependence on the true bread of life, Jesus Christ (John 6:35). We recognize that "breaking of bread" can refer to any meal, but in the Christian context it has special meaning for the communion. Thus whereas Acts 2:46 probably refers to all meals eaten together, the same phrase in 2:42 and 20:7 refers to the communion.

Understanding these terms will enable us more easily to enter into the discussion of communion, appreciating its history while moving toward an understanding that differs from our current practice.

Getting Specific About Communion

What conclusions about communion can we safely draw from the New Testament? Let's approach the subject asking some questions.

Who?

To begin with, exactly who should participate? As you consider the following passages, ask the question, *Who took communion?*

> Those who accepted his message were baptized, and about three thousand were added to their number that day.
>   *They* devoted themselves to the apostles' teaching and to the fellowship, to the breaking of bread and to prayer. (Acts 2:41–42, emphasis mine)

> On the first day of the week we came together to break bread. Paul spoke to the people and, because he intended to leave the next day, kept on talking until midnight. (Acts 20:7)

> Is not the cup of thanksgiving for which we give thanks a participation [*koinonia,* meaning "communion" or "fellowship"] in the blood of Christ? And is not the bread that we break a participation [*koinonia*] in the body of Christ? (1 Corinthians 10:16)

> And when he had given thanks, he broke it and said, "This is my body, which is for you; do this in remembrance of me." (1 Corinthians 11:24)

> So then, my *brothers*, when you *come together* to eat, wait for each other. If anyone is hungry, he should eat at home, so that when you *meet together* it may not result in judgment. (1 Corinthians 11:33–34a, emphasis mine)

It was *Christians* who took the communion. Moreover, there is no evidence from NT times that non-Christians *ever* took the communion. Probably it would not have been especially meaningful to them, since Jesus wasn't *their* Lord. But as for the believers, they were devoted to the Lord's Supper.

What?

Were there any meals that soon-to-be Christians were used to celebrating prior to the institution of the Lord's Supper? Yes—the Old Testament Passover Supper! Understanding the significance of the Passover Supper greatly enhances our appreciation of the Lord's Supper.

Obviously, if one could prove that the Lord's Supper was an extension of the Passover meal into the new covenant—which would be difficult to prove—we would have a strong case for a communion meal. Even though watertight proof cannot be produced, our thinking can certainly be stimulated theologically as we reflect on the possibility. Below are a few observations I've made from Exodus 12 regarding the Passover meal:

- It was a family meal (12:3).
- Smaller family groups could be combined (12:4).
- A reasonable amount of food was determined *in advance*—thus no gluttony (12:4).
- There was a great sense of community—everyone took it at the same time (12:6, 8).
- Passover visibly and concretely reminded Israel of redemption by blood (12:7).
- This was no slow, lazy meal—rather there was a Biblical sense of urgency (12:11).
- With Passover there was no forgiveness of sins—the Passover meal, with the death of the lamb or goat, was only a reminder (12:13, 26). The people's sins were not borne by the Passover lamb or goat.
- Passover was a perpetual ordinance so the people would never forget (12:14).
- There was an explanation of the meal (12:26–27).
- No "guests" were allowed—only Jews and those who had become Jews (12:43–45, 48).
- After the conquest of Canaan, the Passover was to be eaten in one city, Jerusalem, (Deuteronomy 16:5–6) though the feast, for practical reasons, was celebrated in separate groups.
- All covenant members were commanded to be present (12:47). This was no optional or trivial observance.

As for the New Testament communion, a possible implication of 1 Corinthians 11:23–25 is that the breaking of bread initiates the meal. Then, after the meal and to conclude it, the wine (alcoholic, with real C_2H_5OH) is drunk by all. Of course, this is not to say that the "fruit of the vine" might not be commuted to grape juice in the case of recovering alcoholics (Luke 17:1–3, 1 Corinthians 10:13), pregnant women (Judges 13:4–5) and possibly those who cannot drink alcohol as a matter of conscience (Romans 14:23).

> The Lord Jesus, on the night he was betrayed, took bread, and when he had given thanks, he broke it and said, "This is my body, which is for you; do this in remembrance of me." In the same way, after supper he took the cup, saying, "This cup is the new covenant in my blood; do this, whenever you drink it, in remembrance of me." (1 Corinthians 11:23–25)

Either we can say the communion is the meal or that communion is celebrated at the meal. At any rate, it is a fellowship event. Moreover, this is a meal proclaiming Jesus' death until he comes (1 Corinthians 11:26). What an exciting event! Also, and not insignificantly, most Bible commentators believe the original communion was a meal in every sense of the word. It has been argued that Paul *changed* the meal into a token observance, based on 1 Corinthians 11:34. But what does the verse actually say?

> If anyone is hungry, he should eat at home, so that when you meet together it may not result in judgment. (1 Corinthians 11:34a)

Paul isn't forbidding a meal; he is just concerned that all things be done in order and with mutual sensitivity. In other words, "if anyone is [*very hungry, ravenously*] hungry, he should eat at home..."

While it is possible that the Holy Spirit worked through the Corinthians' selfishness to alter the nature of the Lord's Supper from a full meal to an emblematic observance, it is also possible Paul never meant to eradicate the covenant meal as a literal supper.

Would it not be possible to observe the communion as a *fellowship dinner?* Would this be less spiritual than the Protestant version of the Eucharist that we have celebrated in good faith for many years? In fact, it is likely that a "real" meal may actually be a deeper experience since at the table, so to speak, there is nowhere to hide. Meals are spiritual! Of course this isn't to say that every time Christians dine they need to drink wine and celebrate the Eucharist. It is clearly a special celebration.

It could even be said the communion meal is a form of discipling, since Christian conversation naturally tends to focus on spiritual things, our personal lives, exciting news in the kingdom, the "ins" and "outs" of daily evangelism and so forth. The leaders would not have great difficulty sensing, as they looked into the eyes of everyone present, who is doing well spiritually and who needs strengthening, encouragement, warning or prayers. Think of the communion meal as a sort of "Discipleship Group." Instead of an extra meeting, it could to some extent replace an existing meeting.

When?

Choosing when to celebrate the Lord's Supper is up to us. Jesus simply said, "whenever you drink it" (1 Corinthians 11:25). The tradition of Sunday observance is strong and well attested, but there is no command *per se* in the Bible to celebrate communion on a Sunday. The closest we get is Acts 20:7:

> On the first day of the week we came together to break bread. Paul spoke to the people and, because he intended to leave the next day, kept on talking until midnight.... Then he went upstairs again and broke bread and ate. After talking until daylight, he left. (Acts 20:7–8, 11)

The Christians assembled on a Sunday. The question is this: Is an example binding in the absence of a direct command? The onus is on those who would make a command out of an example. Must we eat lamb or goat at the communion meal, eat unleavened bread and bitter herbs, just because Jesus and the apostles did? Clearly not. We should opt for freedom.[2]

Where?

Space is probably the major factor in deciding where to have the communion meal. Any place will do, not necessarily a private upper room, though a private residence will likely afford the hospitality most conducive to celebrating the Lord's Supper.

How?

How should we celebrate the Supper? Should we really try to make it Jewish in tone, à la Seder Supper? How long should it last?

Should we all sit on the same side of the table (for the occasional painter or photographer)? Would we always want a communion talk? Would this be an extra meeting of the body, replace an existing meeting or be some hybrid arrangement? Clearly there are a few details to be worked out. As in many areas of God's will, the nitty-gritty of implementation is left up to us. The Bible doesn't give us a lot on the *How*, but it has more to say about the *Who, What, When* and *Why*.

Why?

Of course communion serves a number of purposes, not just one. It is indeed a remembrance (1 Corinthians 11:24). Naturally, this means it is a time of both great sadness and great joy—sometimes at the same time! There is a profound wisdom in the Lord not dictating exactly how we ought to feel. This way our feelings can be genuine, not manufactured. The congregation is a dynamic system, an ever-shifting matrix of relationships, disappointments, hopes, feelings and responses to the Cross.

Bottom line, I am proposing a communion meal because the potential for spiritual strengthening is great. When we focus on Jesus, we will be stronger in the Lord. It will be harder to fall away, as individuals or as a movement. And anything that increases our focus on Jesus Christ should be seriously considered.

Between Catholic and Correct: Historical Overview

Our present day practice is quite an improvement over the practice of the Catholic church. Yet I would argue that, although for many members our interpretation of communion is quite meaningful, we haven't gone far enough in restoring the Biblical Lord's Supper. This is not to say our communion service is meaningless or unhelpful. I believe it meets a need, but not as powerfully as the fellowship meal that Jesus may have originally intended.

This section has a dual purpose: to enable us to understand in historical context the development of modern Catholic and Protestant notions of communion and, more importantly, to gain some insight into the communion meal in the earliest period of Christianity as instituted by Jesus. A glimpse at the first few generations after the passing of the apostles will be helpful. Four phases will be given superficial attention:

- Early second century
- Mid-second century
- Late second century
- From Reformation to Restoration

Early Second Century

Many first century passages dealing with communion allow us to infer that Christians ate an actual meal and celebrated it regularly. In the early church, Christians often met for fellowship meals (so it seems as we read the New Testament), and evidence indicates that this continued in the second century. Consider for example the letter of Pliny, governor of Bithynia, to the emperor Trajan, approximately 112 AD:

> [The Christians] maintained...that it was their habit on a fixed day to assemble before daylight and recite by turns a form of words to Christ as a god... After this was done, their custom was to depart and to meet again to take food. (Pliny, Epp.X.96.7)

Notice in the passage from Pliny that the meal appears to take place at a *separate* meeting of the body. The dynamic church organizer Ignatius of Antioch (martyred 110–115 AD) wrote to seven churches and often mentions the communion:

> My Desire has been crucified and there burns in me no passion for material things. There is living water in me, which speaks and says inside me, "Come to the Father." I take no delight in corruptible food or in the dainties of this life. What I want is God's bread which is the flesh of Christ, who came from David's line; and for drink I want his blood: an immortal love feast indeed! (Ignatius to the Romans 7:2b–3)

> Try to gather together more frequently to celebrate God's Eucharist and to praise him. For when you meet with frequency, Satan's powers are overthrown and his destructiveness is undone by the unanimity of your faith. (Ignatius to the Ephesians 13:1)

Communion celebrated the right way is powerful! When our focus on Christ is right, God is glorified and the church will be strong.

> Pay close attention to those who have wrong notions about
> the grace of Jesus Christ... and note how at variance they are
> with God's mind. They care nothing about love: they have no
> concern for widows or orphans, for the oppressed, for those
> in prison or released, for the hungry or thirsty. They hold
> aloof from the Eucharist and from services of prayer, because
> they refuse to admit that the Eucharist is the flesh of our Savior
> Jesus Christ... (Ignatius to the Smyrnaeans 7:1)

> Avoid divisions, as the beginning of evil. Follow, all of you,
> the bishop, as Jesus Christ followed the Father; and follow the
> presbytery as the Apostles... Let that Eucharist be considered
> valid which is under the bishop or him to whom he commits
> it... It is not lawful apart from the bishop either to baptize, or
> to hold a love feast. (Ignatius to the Smyrnaeans 8:1–2)

Note that in Ignatius' view no communion was valid unless celebrated under the auspices of the bishop (the chief elder and
overseer).[3] Even as early as the second century we find the seeds
of the later medieval Catholic Church. See also Ignatius to the
Ephesians 20:2, Trallians 2:3, Philadelphians 4:1. (Regarding early
echoes of "transubstantiation" in these citations, see below.)

The *Didache,* or so called *Teaching of the Twelve Apostles,* an
early second century document, gives instructions on communion,
including forms of prayers and who is allowed to partake:

> Now about the Eucharist: This is how to give thanks: First in
> connection with the cup: "We thank you, our Father, for the
> holy vine of David, your child, which you have revealed
> through Jesus, your child. To you be glory forever." Then in
> connection with the piece (broken off the loaf): "We thank
> you, our Father, for the life and knowledge which you have
> revealed through Jesus, your child. To you be glory forever
> ...You must not let anyone eat or drink of your Eucharist
> except those baptized in the Lord's name. For in reference to
> this the Lord said, "Do not give what is sacred to dogs"...
> (Didache 9:1–5)

The "piece" mentioned above may refer to a Jewish custom
whereby the head of the household, after saying a prayer of
thanksgiving, distributed to each of the guests a piece of bread,
broken off a loaf. This is in fact what Jesus did at the Last Supper.
(Of course, it could also mean that less than a full meal was consumed.) Note also that only disciples were admitted to the meal.

The early church seems to have been quite strict about this. Another passage in the Didache reads:

> On every Lord's Day—his special day—come together and break bread and give thanks, first confessing your sins so that your sacrifice may be pure. Anyone at variance with his neighbor must not join you, until they are reconciled, lest your sacrifice be defiled. (Didache 14:1–2)

Sunday was considered by many the best day for the Lord's Supper. This document, like many early Christian documents as well as the entire New Testament, was written in Greek. The Modern Greek word for Sunday is *kyriake,* (from *kyrios,* Lord) is directly translated "the Lord's Day" (Revelation 1:10), the day on which Jesus both rose from the dead and returned in the Spirit at Pentecost.

Mid-Second Century

Now we move one or two generations later and take another look at the church. By the mid-second century, the Christians' understanding of the communion was becoming mystical, bordering on magical. The elements of bread and wine, having been blessed or consecrated, take on a holiness of their own. Read the testimony of Justin Martyr, a Christian intellectual and apologist, around 150 AD:

> We, however, after thus washing [baptizing] the one who has been convinced and signified his assent, lead him to those who are called brothers, where they are assembled...On finishing the prayers we greet each other with a kiss. Then bread and a cup of water and mixed wine are brought to the president of the brothers... When the president has given thanks and the whole congregation has assented, those whom we call "deacons" give to each of those present a portion of consecrated bread and wine and water, and they take it to the absent. (Justin, First Apology, 65)

Water joins bread and wine as a sacred element. (Not to advocate "holy water"!) The elder or bishop who "presides" at the baptism is referred to here as the "president" of the assembly. We see also that communion was the first activity of the newly baptized brother or sister.

> This food we call Eucharist, of which no one is allowed to par-
> take except one who believes that the things we teach are
> true, and has received the washing for the forgiveness of sins
> and for rebirth, and who lives as Christ handed down to us.
> For we do not receive these things as common bread or com-
> mon drink; but as Jesus Christ our Savior being incarnate by
> God's word took flesh and blood for our salvation, so also we
> have been taught that the food consecrated by the word of
> prayer which comes from him, from which our flesh and
> blood are nourished by transformation, is the flesh and blood
> of that incarnate Jesus. (Justin, First Apology, 66)

Once again, only disciples were allowed to share in the Eucharist.
Was this Jesus' intention? Did the early church accurately understand their Master's intent?

Certainly it's encouraging to see that the brothers were still
teaching accurately about baptism. But in the area of communion
they were getting derailed. Reading this paragraph you can see
that we are well on the way to a doctrine of *transubstantiation*.
In its full-fledged form, this doctrine holds that the bread and wine
change *substantially* when blessed by a priest so that they mysti-
cally become the body and blood of the Lord. Continuing in the
passage from Justin:

> And on the day called Sunday, there is a meeting in one place
> of those who live in cities or the county, and the memoirs of
> the apostles or the writings of the prophets are read as long
> as time permits. When the reader has finished, the president
> in a discourse urges and invites us to the imitation of these
> noble things. Then we all stand up together and offer prayers.
> And, as said before, when we have finished the prayer, bread
> is brought, and wine and water, and the president similarly
> sends up prayers... The distribution, and reception of the con-
> secrated [elements] takes place and they are sent to the absent
> by the deacons. Those who prosper, and who so wish, con-
> tribute, each one as much as he chooses to. What is collected
> is deposited with the president, and he takes care of orphans
> and widows, and those who are in want on account of sick-
> ness or any other cause...(Justin, First Apology, 65–67).

Once again, notice the Sunday communion, administered only to
the faithful. It may be that the Christians Justin speaks of held their
communion service as a part of the regular Sunday meeting. We

detect no hard and fast rule on whether communion had to be celebrated separately or not. Yet the devotion of the early Christians to the communion is hard to miss. It was a central element of the Sunday meeting. Finally we see the Sunday contribution for the poor following the communion.

Late Second Century

Irenaeus, writing around the year 190 AD, teaches an even more developed form of Catholic Eucharist:

> For since we are his members, and are nourished by his creation... he declares that the cup, [taken] from the creation, is his own blood, by which he strengthens our blood, and he has firmly assured us that the bread, [taken] from the creation, is his own body, by which our bodies grow. For when the mixed cup and the bread that has been prepared receive the Word of God, and become the Eucharist, the body and blood of Christ.... (Irenaeus, Against Heresies, 3:2–3)

It's a miracle! The bread and wine *literally* become the body and blood of Christ. (Incidentally, this isn't the only area in which Irenaeus sounds like a modern Catholic. His whole attitude toward tradition and the authority of the church is quite Catholic.)

In later centuries, the Eucharist became more and more a spectator event: the congregation was allowed to watch, but was not deemed holy enough to participate. The celebrating priest stood facing the "altar," with his back to the congregation, and continued saying "mass" in Latin long after people had ceased to understand that language.

Even when the "laity" were allowed to partake again, to spill the wine (the blood of Christ) was sacrilege, so only the bread was offered—and that only with a carefully held paten under the chin of the church member lest any crumb fall to the ground, wasted. So much for the religious hocus-pocus. The amazing thing is that its roots are all the way back in the second century—in some ways their communion was closer to the plan of Jesus Christ, in others it was farther off than the modern Protestant notion!

Reformation and Restoration: Halfway to Correct

It is hardly surprising that the Protestant Reformation (sixteenth century onwards) had on its agenda to return the communion to

the people. Groups like the Scottish Church of Christ (1690) celebrated weekly communion. Most Protestant groups celebrate
some form of communion—monthly, annually, bimonthly or at
some other convenient pace.

However dry we insist our feet to be, we must realize that we
stand in the stream of Protestantism. Though independents and
not technically Protestants, much of our thinking about communion is mainline Protestant. The only real point of difference is
that we are accustomed to celebrate communion *weekly,* whereas
other groups fail to see the importance of such regular observance. The Protestant Reformation achieved two crucial things in
regard to communion, and we should not minimize them:

- The bread and wine were returned to the people.
  The illegitimate priesthood lost its grip, and communion was no longer a spectator event.
- Communion was de-mysticized. It returned to "representation"—a vivid symbol of Jesus' sacrifice—not
  "re-presentation" of the sacrifice of Christ.

The Restoration Movement (beginning in the late 1700s), growing out
of the Reformation, went further, adding two more accomplishments:

- Communion was celebrated weekly. I am not here
  arguing that it must be celebrated weekly, but this is
  certainly more the spirit than the typical bimonthly
  or monthly Protestant observance.
- In principle, anyone was allowed to preside over
  communion or do the communion talk. In keeping
  with the broad Protestant principle "priesthood of all
  believers," the false clergy-laity distinction was taken
  out of communion.

How could we come closer still to the plan of God? I propose
two more objectives as we return to the early Christian practice.
After this, our communion (and our joy) should be complete:

- Consider celebrating the communion as part of an
  actual fellowship meal.
- Make the love feast or communion meal a meaningful event for disciples.

At present, in our practice and teaching of the Lord's Supper, we are somewhere between "Catholic" and "correct." If I am on the right track, we are half way there! But why not go all the way? Let's restore the New Testament love feast, the real meal at which the Lord's death was remembered and the participants were strengthened in their communion with Jesus, each other and God the Father.

Implementation

Before we close, an important logistical (and Biblical) question needs to be asked: Is it necessary to observe an actual meal, or is a token observance sufficient? As Christians we gear much of our lives around meals; is another meal really going to cramp our "ministry style"? It would indeed take more time to eat a meal on Sunday evening, for example, than the customary fifteen to twenty minutes devoted to our communion service. But is this a compelling reason to opt for the quick version? Drive-in church services are real timesavers and quite popular in some parts of America. Obviously we would be shocked if someone suggested such a direction for our movement! Yet maybe the apostles might be equally shocked if they saw the current timesaving, quasi-Catholic version of the Lord's "Supper."

In the Old Testament, the people were commanded to take a week out of their normal routine, live in "booths" or tabernacles (*Succoth*), and focus on God. What if the Jews, instead of living under the shelter envisioned in the Biblical command, simply took some palm fronds, attached them to the ceiling and claimed that this fulfilled their duty to observe the Feast of Tabernacles? Every time they looked up and saw the twigs, the thatch or the token "shelter," they would be reminded of the Lord, along with his command to observe Tabernacles.[4]

What if we started reading all of our prayers instead of praying spontaneously? This too would save time. The prayers could be written by eloquent and powerful men and women of God. We could become a liturgical movement. And why not? Because we would be sacrificing a bit of the very heart of prayer and the command to pray (Philippians 4:6). Or what if we started singing just one song per service, relying instead on a choir to artfully sing the other songs? We would have fulfilled our obligation to sing, in a way. But what about the heart of God's intention in the command to sing? (Colossians 3:16). One obvious advantage would be that we probably would not have to fool with songbooks anymore—not to mention those poorly pitched songs! Maybe we could trim our services down to half an hour.

A little sarcasm may help us to see the point: We need to fully implement the commands (both letter and Spirit) of the Lord. Restoration is not a matter of our own convenience. If Jesus had a *supper* in mind, let us get behind having a real meal. And if not, then we should clarify why not.

The history of the church and Israel is chock full of neglect, rationalized by traditions that simplify, circumvent and even nullify the plain teachings of the Bible. The Jews were not careful to observe Passover, Sabbatical and Jubilee years, Tabernacles and other holy days as God intended (2 Kings 23:22, 2 Chronicles 36:20–21, Nehemiah 8:16–17). And, as we all know, the Christians in time also let go of their careful observance of the Lord's commands.

So where do we go from here? Having presented the *Who, What, When, Where, How* and *Why* of a communion meal, together with a historical overview, let me offer some practical suggestions.

- *Make the meal awesome!* If your congregation opts for an actual meal, frame the meal by the Lord's Supper, so that the breaking of bread and prayer begin the meal and taking of wine and prayer end it. If an emblematic observance is preferred, take care to make the meal awesome. As with any other event in the kingdom, planning and effort make the difference between the magnificent and the mediocre.

- *Emphasize quality fellowship* at the meal, not superficial talk nor excessive silence.

- *Don't rush the meal.* The goal isn't to be finished in fifteen minutes.

- *Celebrate in relatively small groups,* especially in homes—by family group, Bible Talk group, discipleship group or neighborhood fellowship.

- *Study out the subject.* Do your own study and come to your own conclusions about the Lord's Supper—for example, who should be allowed to partake and whether the meal was emblematic or a full supper.

- *Overhaul our thinking.* Reconsider everything in a Biblical perspective. A "communion talk" is okay, certainly helpful, maybe essential. We should feel free to experiment and find what works best in our situation, our nation, our culture. (We might even dispense with ushers, golden trays and the micro-cups!)

- *Remove the current "communion service"* from the Sunday meeting. Get rid of the "old yeast"! It will probably be logistically simpler if we meet for communion separate from our main service. If some disciples prefer a more reverent part of the service, maybe add a few worshipful, majestic songs, or sing psalms or reserve a moment for silent prayer.

- *A Sunday evening meal* will likely be convenient for most disciples. Unless we prefer to celebrate it right after the Sunday church meeting.

- *Celebrate the meal often.* Weekly? Well, certainly more often than annually, as in the case of the Passover! Weekly is the implication of Acts 20:7.

- *Should we allow visitors?* My recommendation would be that these small groups exclude visitors. There is no Biblical evidence that guests took the communion, though admittedly there is also no proof they were categorically excluded from the meal. Even Judas seems to have been allowed to take part in the Last Supper—though perhaps not the entire meal. (See also 2 Peter 2:13.) Maybe guests who are "close" to their decision could be allowed to sit in and observe what happens when disciples "break bread" together.[5]

- *What about unleavened bread?* No doubt the Last Supper had unleavened bread—since it was a Passover meal. Yet the case for unleavened bread from 1 Corinthians 5:6–8 is hardly convincing. (Does God have an opinion on this?) At any rate, if we keep using unleavened bread we won't go wrong.

Conclusion

While one cannot prove that the Lord's Supper was invariably an actual meal, still a case can be made for a communion meal, more on the analogy of the Passover meal than the standard Protestant practice. Yet, in the final analysis, devotion to the breaking of bread (Acts 2:42) is not the same to devotion to mere eating. Whether the supper is a table loaded with foods or only emblems loaded with meaning, we are under obligation to remember the Lord. Let us do so.

Notes

[1] The original version was distributed in 1994. In this version I overstated the evidence for an actual "sit-down" meal. Though this is still my leaning, there is certainly a case to be made for the emblematic celebration of the Lord's Supper.

[2] Ironically, it seems in this instance the communion proper was taken on *Monday,* since the meal was eaten sometime between midnight and daybreak. Yet we must be careful how we interpret Acts 20:7. Sunday is the best-attested day (especially from second century writings), yet Monday communion may also have had apostolic approval. Each congregation should be fully convinced in its own mind.

[3] It may concern us to read of "bishops" so soon after the birth of the church. The "bishop" (an anglicized version of *episkopos,* overseer) did not brandish staff and miter, nor swing censers and perform "confirmations." Ignatius' "bishop" is only a slight modification of the NT plan, not the Roman Catholic innovation familiar from high church all the way down to chess set. By the middle of the second century, the "bishop" became the head elder/overseer in each congregation. Later the ruling, or preeminent, bishops ("archbishops") ruled over a whole district of congregations (the area later called the "diocese"). A flexible plan for elders and evangelists had been laid down in the NT writings, yet only eighty years after the resurrection men changed the plan. *So soon?* From our perspective nineteen centuries later, we say, "So soon?" But from another perspective, eighty years is a long time indeed—as great a time span as that between the present and the year 2082! So rather than see swift apostasy in the early church, we should be more positive and see their fidelity for many generations after Jesus Christ's life on earth.

[4] Interestingly enough, modern Jews have given up living in shelters; instead they construct a token structure under which they may spend a few thoughtful moments!

[5] Aren't they drinking judgment on themselves (according to 1 Corinthians 11:29)? Frankly, I don't see how someone who is already lost can become more lost. Still, I would advise that the meal be special—only for Christians.

Who Are We?

Discipleship Publications International (DPI) began publishing in 1993. We are a nonprofit Christian publisher affiliated with the International Churches of Christ, committed to publishing and distributing materials that honor God, lift up Jesus Christ and show how his message practically applies to all areas of life. We have a deep conviction that no one changes life like Jesus and that the implementation of his teaching will revolutionize any life, any marriage, any family and any singles household.

Since our beginning, we have published more than 110 titles; plus, we have produced a number of important, spiritual audio products. More than one million volumes have been printed, and our works have been translated into more than a dozen languages—international is not just a part of our name! Our books are shipped regularly to every inhabited continent.

To see a more detailed description of our works, find us on the World Wide Web at www.dpibooks.org. You can order books by calling 1-888-DPI-BOOK twenty-four hours a day. From outside the U.S., call 978-670-8840 ext. 227 during Boston-area business hours.

We appreciate the hundreds of comments we have received from readers. We would love to hear from you. Here are other ways to get in touch:

Mail: DPI, 2 Sterling Road, Billerica, Mass. 01862-2595
E-Mail: dpibooks@icoc.org

Find Us on the World Wide Web

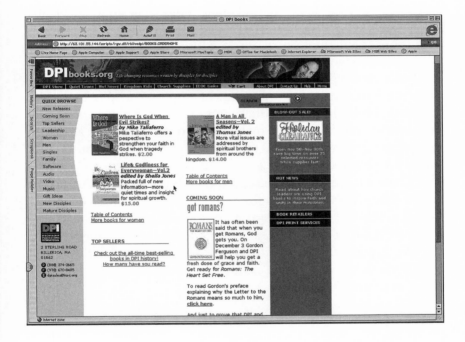

www.dpibooks.org

1-888-DPI-BOOK

Outside the U.S.,
Call 978-670-8840 ext. 227